Evolution of Awareness

KIA MARLENE

Lift Bridge Publishing
Info@liftbridgepublishing.com
www.liftbridgepublishing.com

Lift Bridge Publishing
Waldorf, Maryland
Tel: (888) 774-9917
Printed in the United States of America Publisher's Cataloging-in-Publication data

Cover art by Lau'ren J McGhcc
www.kiamarlene.com
Marlene, Kia

Library of Congress Control Number: 2020906903

ISBN 978-1-64858-005-5

to my parents
lillie and charles
i love you with my whole heart.
thank you so much for everything you've done for me
throughout this journey thus far,
it is greatly appreciated more than you know.

we write
because sometimes the thoughts get heavy in our minds
and we must dispose of them on lines

we write
to get through the confusion
the sadness
and the tough times

we write
so the paper can feel our soul
so those who read what we write
will feel it too

we write
because we are broken
or write for those who are
hoping our words can bandage the scars
and heal them too

we write
to express what our tongues choose not to speak
to allow our hearts to leak
through the ink
onto these sheets
for the world to see

we write
because when our life is full of chaos
only the paper in front of us
and the pen in our hand moving back and forth
can bring us peace

we write
because maybe
just maybe

there's someone out there
who can relate to our words
so we continue to share

we write
because we see our language touching hearts
penetrating minds
so we write some more
because of the change it creates
and because we care

we write
because we have spirit guides and ancestors all around us
who instill their stories into our thoughts
so that they will be told

we write
because *we too* must release stories
thoughts
feelings
and emotions
even if they're old

we write
because the creativity of our minds
and uniqueness of our ideas
wills us to jot these gems down onto paper

we write
because we know the purpose of our thoughts
will impact more than just us
it will impact something greater

we write
to share moments of love
moments of joy

and the bliss we experience

we write
to let go of anger
to let go of sorrow
and the burdens we may be carrying

we write
because this is our therapy
this is our joy
this is our peace

we write
to help ourselves
to help others

and those in need

dedicated to my cousin baby james
and my goddaughter kennedy,
may this book become one of your favorites
once you grow older and are able to understand all that's within
it.

Table Of Contents

The Egg....12
The Caterpillar....71
Intermission (heartbreak&love)....171
The Cocoon....271
The Butterfly....351
Bonus (knock knock)....434
Acknowledgements....442

i am on a journey
a journey that will never end
a journey where i must consistently ask for guidance
a journey where i must ask for strength

it is crucial to be happy
it is crucial to stay focused
it is crucial to think for one's self
and to bloom like a lotus

many won't understand me
and i don't expect them to
many will criticize me
and i'll still respect those who do

all situations
and encounters
i've learned to embrace

all challenges
and fears
i've learned to face

i've discovered peace, joy
and love for all things
i've discovered my purpose, my power
and my divinity

all of these things that i discovered
were already within me and already here
i just had to become available
i had to become aware

on this journey
i am grateful to be on
and thankful for the direction from spirit that is sent

i am on a journey

a journey that will last for eons

a journey that will never end

The Egg

alarm clock going off
it's time to wake up to a higher consciousness
i hit the snooze
what do i have to lose
pulling the covers over me
i'm not ready to wake up

higher self tugging on the covers saying
"get up, rise up"
i roll over and say
"not now, i want more time to finish sleeping"
higher self laughs and says "what is time?
and finish sleeping?
you're sleeping when you're not even in bed
so how about you finally just wake up instead?"

i ask "what's better than being sleep"?
higher self says "a grander you
a grander life
a grander version of reality

a realization of your power
and your divinity
a shift from this linear life
to multidimensional living

to be able to travel from this plane of density
to higher frequencies
to understand your oneness to all
your unity
shall i go on?
are you yet feeling me?

you are the reason for forever
but you won't realize this
if you choose to be sleeping for forever

you are an unlimited entity
who is a spiritual being
whose flesh is not its true identity

did you know you're more than matter?
while down here hitting the snooze button
like waking up don't matter

haven't you heard the phrase
when you snooze you lose?
well let's start winning
and get this veil of illusion
from thick to thinning
then from thinning to lifted

i'm here to guide

you down to ride?

the things that i'm saying are you yet with it?

so wipe that crust out your eye
and let's decalcify that crust on your third eye

let's awake to create
let's awake to activate
let's awake so you and i can rise and integrate."

time's up
alarm clock goes off again
i didn't hit the snooze this time
i press stop

i tell myself

it's time to wake up

q. what is your definition of the higher self?

a. the higher self to me is the true self, the authentic self, a multidimensional intelligence, the one that guides, the one that knows all, the one that knows what we will experience before we experience it. our higher self knows the many roads we will take before we even take them, our higher self knows our purpose, it's a part of us, it's the highest aspect of us, beyond the physical, beyond the 3rd dimension, our higher self is unlimited and eternal. our link to our higher self is always there and available, and it can be a strong or weak link depending on our awareness, our frequency and how in tune we are. our higher self wants the best for us, it's always contacting us and wanting to connect with us. our higher self is one we must trust. it has all the answers, it has all the knowledge and once we build our faith in our higher self all of its services will be available for us. then, life will make more sense. trust what lies inside, trust all that you are, trust your higher self and allow it to guide you effortlessly.

sometimes there's a victory waiting for you once you surrender

Kia Marlene

they say time heals all wounds
but i thought time didn't exist
so who or what will heal these wounds?
because right now i'm too weak to even clean them
let alone bandage them up and allow them to mend

i'm too tired to be strong
my mind has been carrying the weight of aches and pains
from many lives before mine
those which my soul has occupied
and that my body currently can feel

and every time i cry it's like my face is full of open sores
and these tears are made of wray and nephew
because it hurts

it hurts because crying didn't release anything this time
but emotional pain that chose to linger in my body and my mind
emotional pain from a time when the hurt was physical
i can't remember
but the pain remembers me

i don't ask why me or why this life
there may be other versions of myself
so i ask why this version
what exactly is stored in me that caused trauma, damage
or torture to my existence that is causing me to feel it now?

this pain
these wounds
i no longer want to feel
so if anybody is listening tell me how

because i'm confused
and i'm at a loss for words
i'm feeling pain from situations i don't recall experiencing

so "how can i heal?"
i need an answer to these four words

so my mind
body
and soul
can move forward

because right now i feel drained
i feel like i can't go on anymore
and i don't know where i'm going or where i started

so if time heals all wounds and time doesn't exist
am i meant to heal during this lifetime?
or did i choose to experience a life where i don't
because my strength level is at a zero
and i honestly feel like i won't

maybe i was way too strong in other lifetimes
and maybe i have to be a lot less strong in this one
to balance things out

maybe i've been fighting for centuries
and i picked this life to not fight
maybe i picked this life to not heal and to just be

because right now i have no fight in me
and i'm ok with that

right now i have no fight in me
and i'm ok with that

at least for now

fake aches
fake pain
pain is only in the mind
but how can i get this pain out of my mind
so i don't have to feel it in my body?
my mind is my body
so i guess i'm experiencing a mental cleanse

mind body one right?
mind body one right?

each cough my head hurts
each sneeze phlegm is released
sneezing is an unconscious act
so does that mean my soul is purging?
eyes are the window to the soul
so what is happening to what i'm seeing?
i asked for more information to be revealed
and clarity on the info that was already stored within me
i guess the mind had to make room and the body did too

or is the soul healing?
is the mind shedding?
exfoliating consciousness?
because my skin is peeling

mind body one right?
mind body one right?

as mucus is being coughed up am i coughing up limited
thoughts, or burdens on my soul from old days?
or messed up patterns and habits from old ways?
am i coughing up the prison keys that kept my mind locked?
or the illusionary watch that made my growth temporarily stop?

purging foreign matter that don't matter?

becoming available for my consciousness to climb ladders?

mind body one right?
mind body one right?

is this cleanse that i'm experiencing a cleanse that is not only
healing but allowing me to remember my power and who i am?
allowing me to realize that i am divine
powerful
and a creator like i am?

fake aches
fake pains
pain is only in the mind
but how can i get this pain out of my mind
so i don't have to feel it in my body?
whispers in my ears saying
"you will get through this too"

whispers in my ears saying

"you will get through this too"

when i thought i had nothing
i soon realized
i had everything

Kia Marlene

dear winter 2016
not sure what to make of this
wish i can hide this
cover this all up
wish i can conceal and makeup this

whatever the cause was
with a little determination
i know i can make up this

from all good just a week ago
to all confusing
i swear
i can't make up this

i was doing so well
positive affirmations
and feeling good inside
then things went left
and i wasn't quite prepared for that ride

i yearned for more money
but funds kept running low
one thing led to another
then i found myself back on winslow

wasn't ready for a 9-5
just started learning about my power
so i decided not to go back to that life
but what i experienced was not what i wanted
so i had to learn more of my power so it can be utilized

i felt like i was moving backwards and not forwardly
i'm thinking to myself "is this really what's for me"?

i mean i could've gone harder with my hobby
turned hustle
turned passion
turned back to hustle
but i got tired of that

so i had to pack up
trust the process
do some soul searching
and evaluate my world to see where i was really at

the questions i asked myself were
"what is my purpose"?
"why am i here"?
"and for my still unknown plan how can i prepare"?

see i needed my conscious clear
separated from the outside world because i needed answers here
i know the answers are out there somewhere
then i heard a voice say "not out there but inside my dear"

not afraid to embrace my emotions
so yes, i shed a few tears
spirit dried them up
i'm divinely guided
i knew my guides cared

i had nothing to fear
but first i had to ask "is clarity, prosperity and inner peace near?
i know life is a journey but right now can abundance and wealth
be spared"?

then i heard the universe say "first get to know your soul
rediscover your road
love earth and take care of her
learn how life work

then abundance and wealth will greatly be spared"
then it hit me
i thought i was going backwards
but really i was moving forward
higher self probably like
if only she knew what was in store for her

i realized that this interruption of happiness to confusion
was a part of my assignment
i had to hide within this dark place to bring about enlightenment
i realized i had to take full responsibility for where i'm at
and embrace all of this journey
i knew that all i wanted was on the other side of trusting where
i'm at currently

so i intend to accept this new chapter
this new phase
this new season
and all that's occurring for me

dear winter 2016
i may not have understood what was going on at first

but i thank the spirit of transformation for choosing me

q. i found myself back on winslow?

a. yes, winslow is one of the streets i grew up on. winslow is where my mom house is located. i found myself moving back home (and luckily for me her upstairs apartment was vacant (laughs)), but it was in that moment i found myself moving backwards, and no one wants to move back home once they've left. it was a very humbling experience for me and i was stubborn at first but i accepted what was happening and that was huge for me. i learned to accept the change even though it wasn't the change i wanted to experience. i eventually learned that every setback is not a setback.

the girl before the hurt
the girl before the pain
the girl before the storm
the girl before the rain

she still exists

the girl before the tears
the girl before the wounds
the girl who used to care
the girl before bad moods

she still exists

the girl before the frowns
the girl who wore her crown
the girl who had a voice
and was never feeling down

she still exists

the girl who thought for herself
the girl before insecurity
the girl who used to have fun
and didn't try to fit in with the majority

she still exists

the girl who used to smile
the girl who used to love
the girl who knew joy
the girl who knew trust

she still exists

the girl who had passion

the girl who used to laugh
the girl who loved her reflection
and didn't care what others thought of her when asked

she still exists

the girl who had inner peace
the girl who forgave
the girl who light shined
and didn't allow her self-esteem to sink in and cave

she still exists

the girl who was a stranger to depression
the girl who didn't let doubt whisper in her ear
the girl who didn't worry
the girl who didn't fear

she still exists

the girl who was motivated
the girl who used to explore
the girl who used to imagine
the girl who, for herself, wanted more

she still exists

because all she has to do is remember
re-live
and search within

to whom it may concern

she still exists

welcome her back

it’s easy to suppress our emotions
but it takes strength to address and release them

Kia Marlene

this time i will let these tears flow
no more wiping
no more hiding
i won't go outside in the rain
i will let these tears rain on my cheeks down to my chin

i will let it rain on my collarbone
and all over my skin

i will allow my flesh to feel these tears
i will allow my emotions to overflow without care

they say crying cleanses the soul
so i will cry until no more tears are being produced
and if i have to i will cry all day long

i will let it all out
and free these tears from the jail cells
of me trying to be way too strong

i will not be ashamed
i will embrace this meaningful waterfall that flow from my eyes
i will not touch these tears
i will let them come in contact with the spirits of the ether so that
they can air dry

i will not dwell in this tear producing emotion
yet i will cleanse
question it
and try to further inner-stand the purpose of this moment

it will no longer be me versus my feelings
i will no longer be my emotions opponent

so if you think crying makes you weak

i want you to guess again
because the only thing that makes you weak
is not allowing yourself to heal from within

cry

change came
and left its stain
expanding the domain
i won't complain
i won't refrain
grateful for the gain
even if its reason is one the conscious mind has yet to obtain

change came
and revised the game
dissolving the same
sparking new flames
giving the old a new name
old habits, bitter it came

change came
bringing confusion and pain
creating emotional drain
preventing the ego from killing the spirit like abel and cain
comfort is slain
subconscious retrain
alarming the brain
breaking the chain

change came
causing a switch in lanes
a shift in planes
no avoiding it like non-smokers catching contact from the smoke
of mary jane
calling change insane
when it's here to keep souls at peace and sane
penetrating membranes
holding you up like a cane
intending to be major
(no payne)

change came
with no reason to explain
no need to restrain
i'll embrace and have faith the size of a fonio grain
staying positive is my aim
knowing the sun shines after the rain
hoping this change is not in vain
hoping this change makes me available for higher awareness
attained

change came

i became so obsessed with the law of attraction
that i didn't realize there were other laws
i had to understand

Kia Marlene

i gave positivity my best shot
but i just couldn't keep the feelings of non-positivity down
they floated to the surface in my sea of confusion
i felt betrayed by the law of attraction as i realized i was getting
nothing of what i was putting out
and these positive affirmations was doing nothing for me
but bringing me to a place i was trying to avoid

"i am happy
i am healthy
i am prosperous
i am wealthy"

what does this all mean if i'm not experiencing what i speak?
should i continue to still sound like a robot
hoping these repetitive statements change what i see?

because right now it's hard to feel wealthy
whenever the atm machine reminds me of my balance
and i can't say i feel happy and healthy
when everyday i'm stressing about low funds
which is manifesting headaches instead of cash
everything still seems out of balance

i was tired of hearing about divine timing
what about my timing?
because i need happiness
health
and wealth
to come find me

so tell me when do these positive affirmations start to kick in?
because right now i feel like they're laughing at me
when can i experience these affirmations in the physical
so i can feel as though they're finally backing me

eventually i said forget these affirmations
it's time to accept where i'm at currently
it's time to stop being delusional
while negative thoughts try to bury me

it's time to discover what i'm supposed to learn from this lesson
and accept the now
i finally embraced how i truly felt and asked for a way out
but i'm still wondering how

affirmations turned into questions
as i kept it real about how i felt
questions like "how can i release what no longer serve me?
and what do i have to do to heal?
how can i change my low vibrations to high?
and how can i utilize the power of my intent and will?

how can i change confusion to clarity?
and lack to prosperity?
how can i become a better version of myself
so i can affect those who are near to me?

how can i make myself available for growth
and activate what the cells already know?
because i'm realizing evolution and transformation
need to be the goal"

questions got answered
as i chose not to fight the dark and the confusion
but instead allowed it to be my teacher and my friend
spirit gave me the answers to everything
and taught me how to manifest
but it first showed me how to go within

i no longer covered up scars i didn't understand
i decided to transform and allow healing

so that they can turn into new skin

no longer avoiding the avoidable
embraced each emotion and feeling without judgement
told myself this has got to be the key to win

i became ready for life lessons
squared off with the toughest of them
and told them "i will master you
finish you
and then i will overstand you"
and at this point i'm realizing the message from the universe
and my guides had finally gotten through

i had to get shaken up by the universe
get in tune and learn some things new
i had to remember the purpose of my journey
and stay to it very true

i became so obsessed with the law of attraction
that i didn't realize there were other laws to understand
became so obsessed with just wanting to manifest a bunch of money

didn't realize my higher self had better plans

distilled waters leaking
from the windows of my soul
this time i let them be

i choose not to disrupt the flow
with my hands
shirt
or soft tissue
i choose to let them leak

for once i don't suppress
i just express
and let them lead

i'm tired of pinning down my emotions
like a wrestler in a ring
and not hearing myself tap out and count to three

for once
the tears that water from my eyes
i don't hide

i just let them be

we bottle up our emotions
but never pour them out

Kia Marlene

so i screamed out what i was available for
no longer whining about what i wanted
and what i needed

i made my intentions clear
wrote the words from my mind as they appeared
and visualized for added energy once everything was seeded

i no longer blamed the outside world
for my situations
experiences
and unexplainable events

i took full responsibility for all that i created
because i know that leads to the road of self-empowerment

i realized how grand i am
and the value of my being
i realized how divine my 3d experience is
and that everything has a deeper meaning

i no longer stressed
complained
or became aggravated
all i did now was see the good in everything
smiled and laughed more
keeping my mind and mood elevated

because i perceived the world as safe and beautiful
a safe and beautiful world is what i experienced
and because i commanded health and well-being over my body
health and well-being is what i experienced

i no longer cried tears of frustration
sadness
anger or confusion

instead i trusted each moment
while asking for guidance to see pass the illusion

i no longer searched outside myself
for healing that needs to take place within
i now make myself available for any
and all transformation to truly begin

i no longer entertained thoughts of fear, worry or doubt
those things no longer receive my energy
thoughts i entertain now are of love
joy
happiness
inner peace and prosperity

i no longer struggle
i no longer overthink
i now attempt to see the bigger picture
and understand the purpose of all things

i continue to smile
i continue to keep the faith

and i continue to express gratitude for everything

why does it sound like i'm the only one here
for a minute there was silence
and only children's laughter i would hear
is this world made just for me?
should i start listening close and be more observing?
beetle noises from trees
buses with angel numbers on them riding by
conversations with a man who was sleeping on the bench
who seemed like he was from a different reality
or a different lifetime

i looked up

and strangely no birds in the sky

on this journey
i must learn to love myself enough
to let go of all that isn't love

Kia Marlene

how many times will it take for me to be over you
until i'm finally over you?
last month i was over you
now i'm up under you
last week i was over you
now i'm running back over to you
how many times will it take for me to be over you
until i'm finally over you?
5
10
15 times
maybe 20
friends asking me *"how many chances have you given him"*
i reply "20 times plenty"
how many times will it take for me to be over you
until i'm finally over you?
maybe when love for self stop being stagnant at the sacral
and i allow it to rise up over you
expressing and showing love for all of me is really long overdue
i wish this so-called thing of ours had a better overview
how many times will it take for me to be over you

until i'm finally over you?

why is my soul tied to you?
i want to untangle it out of this knot
i can't continue to grow and evolve
and be attached to someone who is not

your energy is no longer welcome within my thoughts
your aura is no longer welcomed into my space
your vibrations can no longer emit into my field
i no longer want to see you in my face

wait

i'm almost done untangling this knot
and when i do
i'm throwing this rope of attachment out where no one can trace
i've learned my lesson
you we're a test that i retook
but have finally aced

it's over now
get off of me
i will not touch nor tease you like case
i don't want to see you again
and you are not welcomed back like mase

this knot has been untangled
and the soul is no longer tied to you

and when i see you in the streets

my conscious mind won't even say hi to you

i want to put overthinking in a casket
and bury it 6ft under
and there will be no funeral services
for anyone that wonders

i will bury it before it buries me
i took away its right to reincarnate in my life
so it will be in the waiting room for another

overthinking out here ruining the gift of the present
encouraging us to forget that now is the gift
the present

focusing on non-existent nows
worrying
indulging in anxiety
over analyzing
making our cells age faster than they should

trying to inner think instead
because overthinking is dead
r.i.p.

anything other than the now
and thoughts that don't give me peace
happiness
or make me calm
i will no longer give it my energy

i'm done filling up my mind with
"i should've
what ifs
and i shouldn't"

creating imaginary problems
when i know that i shouldn't

overthinking has ran its course through the tracks of my mental
i'm putting overthinking to rest and it will be non-accidental

so cheers to overthinking
thank you for the experience
but you will not be missed

my new mindset is having a party

and you are not a guest on the list

leave me alone
it's over
we're done here
stop trying to reach me
stop trying to get in my mind
i don't want to hear your whispers in my ear
you've set me back long enough
i must let you go
i'm strong enough
i don't need you
nor want you
i've outgrown you
i'm not weak no more
i won't allow you back into my space
you can't stare into my eyes
no more of you on my face
i've found the courage to move on and i know i deserve the best
letting you go during this journey was indeed the very best
get off of me
stop trying to pull me back into your world
i'm not who i was anymore
i am not that girl
you didn't win this time
i'm not turning back this time
i gave you too many of my thoughts and have entertained
enough of your energy
time's up
you get no more time
at least not of mine
you being back with me is the last thing on my mind
i'm over you
and there's nothing you can do to make me miss you
i'm over you
and there's nothing you can do to make me not dismiss you
i gave you enough of me and the life we had is now finished
fear

i want no more parts of you

your existence in my world has been diminished

i refuse to work for a corporation
i refuse to fulfill someone's 9-5
i refuse to allow my dreams to be deferred for a pay check
from a company that wouldn't care if next week i wasn't alive

i refuse to ignore my creativity
which indeed lies inside
i refuse to not imagine my desires
and not watch them materialize

i refuse to suppress my purpose, passions and powers
and not let them shine
i refuse to be in the backseat of my world
and not be the one who drives

i refuse to settle for mediocrity
when i was born to thrive
i refuse to stand on the shore of infinite possibilities
and not take a dive

i refuse to choose average
and not give greatness a try
i refuse to sit and do nothing
while the train of legendary
passes me by

i refuse to be anything less than extraordinary
extraordinary which is i
i refuse to not display my grandness
and not benefit from the powers of my mind

i refuse to not know and realize
that i am greater and divine
i refuse to settle for less

and not make the most of my time

q. oh, so you refuse?

a. yup (laughs), that was my mood while i was writing that poem. can't recall what triggered it but that's how i've been feeling since i quit my last full-time job. i just wanted more for myself, i wanted to do more and be more, and i wanted to create something and enjoy whatever i did and do it with love. at that time i wasn't quite sure what it would be (laughs) but i knew i didn't want to be clocking in anywhere anymore. i knew it was more in store for me, i knew i had a greater purpose than working a 9-5 and i wanted to devote my time and energy to figuring out what that was.

q. are you against 9-5's?

a. no no no not at all, trust me i had plenty of 9-5s, 3-11s, 2-8s, 5-10s (laughs) but at the end of the day you have to make sure that you truly love what it is you're doing, make sure you leave a great impact and always ask yourself "is this a part of my purpose," and never let your job drain you of your energy.

if your heart is not in it then don’t do it
because it’ll drain your energy
rather than add to it

Kia Marlene

if doubt and worry were liquefied within a 2-liter bottle
i'm twisting open that cap
i'm pouring it out
while saying *"this ain't for me or my homies"*

i'm crushing up the bottle
because i don't care about getting that nickel back
it's time to say goodbye

photograph

nickelback

no longer will you be on my taste buds
matter of fact i've become allergic
doubt and worry for you
i have the strongest aversion

ok scratch that
i won't go that far
you can't get my energy like that
because from you i'm taking my energy right back

i will no longer drink you
you will no longer have a place in my refrigerator of peace
your taste has become bitter
i spit you out
no longer are you sweet

your low vibrational frequency is no longer a match for me
you won't taste right with my meals of confidence and serenity

so if doubt and worry were liquefied within a 2-liter bottle
i'm twisting open that cap
i'm pouring it out
while saying

this ain't for me or my homies

where do my thoughts go when i'm thinking?
who or what is processing the images that i'm seeing?
who else can feel these feelings that i'm feeling?
other than god who else can hear me if i decide to pray
and start kneeling?

besides what i'm aware of
what else is this universe concealing?
how can i become available to all of its information?
how can i become aware of what its revealing?

how can i assist earth with her well-being
and all of her that needs healing?
what do i have to change about myself
in order for my vibration to be high
to make my ancestors and spirit guides proud
and for my energy to be appealing?

how can i become a better version of myself
and shed off old skin?
how can i release my true self?
what's the best way to start my search within?

how can i know more of my soul
and understand the thoughts that come to the mind?
are there other versions of me
in a different space
and a different lifetime?

if time is man-made
is this 3d plane the only place where it's acknowledged?
if i need to know thyself
then what's really the point of college?

what if nature can talk to us
but we have to raise our frequency to understand it?

how can i become available for more love
and more light?
and for more transformation?

is watching tv a form of frequency control?
are there subliminal messages on the tv beyond the screen that
we don't know?
is the body held together by sound?
if so how can i get myself in tune and become one with the flow?

is my subconscious mind programmed by symbols, repetition
emotions and attitudes?
do my cells have consciousness?
and are they really intelligent?

so dna isn't controlled by biology?
my genes aren't my destiny?
environmental influences can modify genes?
and all that *"it's genetics"* talk is irrelevant?

is there really no cause of anything?
what more should i know about my dharma?
for better health and awareness
should i start by being conscious of my breathing?
and is there a connection between the human ego and karma?

am i here on earth to gain experience
learn lessons and collect wisdom?
is reincarnation real?
when people pass on should i not cry or miss them?

is missing anyone who has departed
keeping me in bondage to the past?
don't the deceased continue on and return to the vast?

why do they call it death?

doesn’t the spirit just experience rebirth with a new body?
don’t we just change forms?

do we always reincarnate with the same family members?

will my great-grandfather be my first born?

who am i?

am i kia?
does my name mean anything when i've been here before?
who am i inside this human body?
how many people have i been?
how many times have i come back?
what cultures have i explored?

who am i?

do my thoughts belong to me?
who or what am i tuned into?
is this mine, or someone else's identity?

who am i?

are there other versions of myself?
what has my soul experienced?
do i really know thyself?

who am i?

am i my thoughts?
my reflection?
my mood?
my perceptions?

who am i?

how can i know more of my soul?
how can i remember what i already know?
how can i understand this road?

who am i?

what is my purpose?
what is my role?
am i guided on which way to go?
how much am i a part of the whole?

who am i?

does what i do affect the environment?
do limited thoughts affect my intelligence?
does my perception affect my empowerment?

who am i?

so i'm not flesh?
i'm energy?
a spirit inside a human body with sensory?
made up of cells consisting of cellular memory?

who am i?

if energy can't be destroyed then am i immortal?
is this human body just a vehicle?
a machine?
a portal?

who am i?

do the things i experience and don't understand
make sense in another life?
if i search within will my soul bring things to light?

who am i?

am i light?
a collection of thoughts?
collective consciousness?

a collection of individuals?
is my evolution and maturation really pivotal?

who am i?

am i a thought in god's mind?
am i really made in god's image?
when i look into the mirror am i looking into god's eyes?

who am i?

different body, same soul?
same trip, different road?

who am i?

why did i choose to exist on earth?
why did i choose this journey?
am i everyone and is everyone me?

who am i?

am i all that there is
here to gain wisdom and experience a spiritual evolution?
how can i receive clarity on who i am
what more is there to learn about myself?
and if lack of self-awareness is the problem

then what's the solution?

what if the next millennium is already happening
what if a year ago was yesterday
what if 5 years from now is the next hour
what if last month was the next century
what if 20 minutes ago was the last decade
what if 15 years from now was a week ago
what if the next minute was the next day

and what if all of this was happening now?

illusion or real
friend or foe
control or freedom
do we worship time?
are we slaves to it?
does anybody know?
abundant or scarce
welcomed or feared
man-made or of god
does what we perceive as time
or our awareness of it
lock us up in bondage
to prevent us from experiencing spiritual evolution
and divine growth?
can we feel time?
can we see time
other than when we look at a clock?
what is time's purpose?
to speed things up?
or
on a deeper level
make things stop?
to be grateful for it?
or to desire a world where it doesn't exist?
to shun it?
or appreciate it?
to reflect upon it?
or dismiss all thoughts of it?
understood or misunderstood
solid or flexible
beneficial or no need
are we prisoners of time?
if so how can we be freed?
simultaneous or linear
experienced in other realities
and dimensions

or just this one
past
present
future
aren't they all happening now?

aren't they all one?

if age isn't real and time is an illusion
then i assume communication is still open with my younger self
so i talk to her
tell her that she's loved
tell her to be strong throughout all of her experiences
if nothing else

if age isn't real and time is an illusion
then my younger self still exists
at least that's what i concluded
i tell her life is a game that she will learn how to play
i root for her and tell her that she can do this

i communicate with her by talking to her pictures
or corresponding through letters
i tell her that she's beautiful and things will get better

i tell her that she's wise
and to anticipate her rise
and that everything she wants is already hers
just imagine, believe and visualize

i tell her that she's intelligent
far more than she knows it
i tell her to love and embrace who she is
and don't be afraid to show it

if age isn't real and time is an illusion
then can i heal disturbing experiences
that have occurred before now?
can i resolve unresolved issues and bring forth forgiveness
that i previously didn't allow?
if i can't change what happened can i alter my perception of it?
will that modify the emotions stored in my subconscious mind?
will that remove any deception of it?

if age isn't real and time is an illusion
then is communication open with my future self?
can i be available for her words and guidance if nothing else?
can she offer me information
that i can use in this current moment?
can she give me the vision to notice the signs
see the bigger picture
while keeping my spiritual eyes open?

if age isn't real and time is an illusion
then i know my future self must exist
and i think i recall her speaking to me
she heard my concerns and came forth to bring clarity

she said "whatever you encounter or go through is there to teach
you and help you grow
there's no such thing as a wrong path
you are on the right road

it's not what you go through
it's how you go through it
you have within you the power
make yourself available and learn how to use it

you are extremely healthy
wealthy
and indeed divine

just continue to love your body
yourself
and of course your life

you are guided
and things always end up being fine
don't be hard on yourself
stay focused

and be aware of the thoughts that come to your mind

you know a lot
but you will learn a lot more
you know you are grand
but you will soon find out that you are much grander than you know

be open for knowledge
be open to growth
don't see challenges as challenges
see them as lessons from the soul

you are wise
and will continue to rise
and everything you want is already yours

just continue to imagine, believe and visualize

we are all reincarnated consciousness
inside a new vessel that we chose
the question is
do we truly know who we are inside of this vessel?
do we know all of what we experienced before this moment?
can we remember the memories our soul stored for us?
why did we choose this body?
why did we choose this lifetime?
why this journey?
why earth?
why here?
why now?

ask yourself
who am i?

and what is it that i came here to do?

now i lay me down to sleep
asking my higher self to send information to me
information that will equip me
for the following day
the following rising
information that will reassure me
that i am divinely guided

if i shall wander in thought, before i sleep
i give my higher self permission to redirect
if i encounter anything less than love and light
i give my higher self permission to intercept

i trust my higher self
i love my higher self
i am truly grateful for the guide

now i lay me down to sleep
relaxing peacefully in the now

handing my cares over to the most high

q. how do you feel, right here, right now, in this moment?

a. i feel like there's a transformation occurring and i intend to allow it to happen. i intend for this transformation to have an impact on more than just myself and i intend to share all that i experience with the world. i intend for my talent of sharing my journey through poetry to assists others with their own journeys, and that talent is one i intend not to waste.

lorenzo said the saddest thing in life is wasted talent
so i grabbed a pen and some paper
and wrote all thoughts that were valid

i started to stop
look
and listen to my surroundings
took my shoes off
felt earth's surface
and started grounding

i allowed information to come towards me
and through me
as i resonated with all that my soul mentioned
i learned from books
documentaries
nature
and of course intuition

this knowledge i was accumulating
i had to start sharing
the future of earth and humanity
i quickly started caring
everything i experienced i had to take note
i asked myself questions
trusted spirit
and was grateful for all that i know

this journey i could not hide it
my transformation could not be silent
this path that i chose
i am indeed happy to be guided

so if my talent is sharing thoughts
from my journey
through poetry

then no
it did not go to waste

i intend for all things that i'm expressing
to motivate
inspire
and bring about change

The Caterpillar

how can i help heal the pain of the ancestors
that live through me?
how can i help heal the pain so this pain
won't pass down genetically?
i want to help assist the healing of my ancestors
because the real revolution happens through the cells
and if my ancestors live through me
then the real revolution is through myself

how can i help?

transformation is happening
i can feel it in my body
so i know that it must also be happening in my mind

i'm grateful for every emotion that rise to the surface
every thought that makes me nervous
every pain that aches
and i wish was hurtless
every part of this transformation serves a purpose

so i will indulge in the unknown
the uncertainty
and the unseen

i will rejoice for the light that i do not yet feel
and the dark that currently covers me

because it's all energy
it's all a part of the inner me

trying to block out negativity
so it can no longer enter me
trying to inner stand the ego
so i can no longer call it the enemy

learning and loving all of my soul
while welcoming all that it reveals to me
trusting my higher self and this journey
while remaining cool and witnessing myself transform ever so
splendidly

reminding myself that i am grand
i am divine
i am indeed

a sovereign entity

transforming me
is transforming my ancestors
because they still live
they live through me

Kia Marlene

spoke to my ancestors
and told them i will heal for us
i will do what i have to do
i will use my intent and will for us

if my ancestors chose me
then i will act and not be still for us
i will use my courage and call out for the darkness
to be revealed for us

when darkness is revealed
it brings an opportunity to heal
so no more misuse of energy running through the field for us
if healing is hidden under layers of dark
then layers i will peel for us

if i have to request for the wounds
pain
fear
unhealthy patterns
and dis-ease of the human psyche
deep down within our being and genes
to rise to the surface
then i will make that appeal for us

inner-standing the dark is necessary
so if the dark begins handing out plates
then i will eat this meal for us
can't reach the light
without knowing and going through the dark
so i will experience it and feel for us

i won't run from darkness
i will go toe to toe with it
while learning its lessons and secrets
all while cleansing this ill for us

because i intend to heal deep generational wounds
no neosporin

healing me and all ancestors

ancestors from the celestial
even those that seem foreign

people say do it for the culture
well i'm doing it for my cells

i'm doing it for my genes
my biological line
those before and after me
i'm doing it for our health

and any unpleasant stains we may have left in the ether
assisting in this vibrational shift
allowing our energy to penetrate further and deeper

revitalizing our existence and frequency
that affects the astral and above

healing the dark

introducing it to love

i no longer want to be a product of the fear that's stored in the
cells of my ancestors
so i invited healing to my temple
it's time to pop and squeeze out the swollen imprints of horror
that was left on the depth of my consciousness
treating fear like a pimple

if my ancestors live through me
we need to heal through me
so let the healing begin
any multidimensional ancestors?
let the healing extend

memories of trauma
that accumulated in the cells of my ancestors
to heal i will take full responsibility
any wounds that rise to the surface
i will embrace them
understand them
be strong and prepare myself for any possibility

if my ancestors live through me
i intend to heal what we never could heal
i desire to settle unresolved emotional issues
i intend to feel what we never could feel

conscious of my breathing
i inhaled joy and exhaled despair
conscious of my breathing
i inhaled freedom and exhaled fear

landlord of my temple
i told my ancestors it's time for fear to get evicted
we will utilize our power
know who we are
around here consciousness will be shifted

so if my ancestors live through me
and their story runs through my rich bloodline
it's time to purify any unpleasant energy that circulates my being
so that we can shine

we will record this on our genes
are own truth
without limits
new beliefs
changed perceptions
fear has lost the game and left the scene

we claim power
renewed strength
and now bravery from us is what they see

i told fear to pack up and leave
and to never touch the trillion of cells
that make me we

Kia Marlene

i'm wanted in another dream
they tugging on me before i sleep
i'm dozing off unexpectedly
ancestors active in my unconscious aggressively
trying to get me to remember my purpose
so i can carry it out effectively
trying to tell me tales about my lineage
so i can embrace who i am successfully
i'm observing dreams within dreams
finding out that things ain't what they seem
i just experienced 5 lifetimes within a 5 minute nap
i just received 5 downloads without downloading apps
i'm wanted in another dream

i think it's time to go back

what does this all mean?
why are we here?
what is my purpose on this planet earth?
i mean plane, dimension?

children spin their fingers on a globe
but no one says anything about a dome
no one mentions that gravity may just be someone's theory
a theory that made people believe
and therefore made it seem real

no one mentions why we are taught to say good morning
when there is nothing good about mourning
unless we're living in a dead world
or why they tell us to have a good weekend
when i'd rather stay strong
telling us to be blessed
when i'd rather be more

telling us to pray to jesus christ
but i'd rather not kill my imagination
the creative power
the animator that gives life like the sun
i'd rather not prey to anything

yet children are taught to sound it out

living in a black hole
the divine feminine can feel my sole
because rarely will there be unconducive material in between us
as this realm we experience is in between the feminine
and the masculine
the division symbol
father above
mother beneath us

and if we are living in the shadow realm
and this body is a shadow of my spirit
i will ingest lightly
and not allow food to be heavy inside my main brain
so that when the spirit speaks i will hear it

and if there is indeed a trinity
how dare we leave out the divine feminine
the goddess who can help our intents come to fruition
creator of all things is she
experiencing life on her territory is we
and i rather inner-stand than understand
and maybe i'll start with trying to inner-stand
why every time i fast from food
the ringing in my ears get louder and last longer

or maybe i'll try to overstand how the moon may not be original
but was placed here
and is owned and controlled by beings who may live inside
and extract energy instead of give energy like the sun
but i still love the moon with all that i am
because all that i am is a part of the one

but what is original anymore?
they are calling produce organic that has no seeds
and when i eat only fruit my womb barely bleeds

so tell me what is original?
earth which is my body
fire which is my soul
air which is my breath
water which is my feelings
and spirit which i am and immersed in

we are the elements
we are the creators

we are the divine
clones of the infinite
but worshipping the god of time
accepting almost anything that is slipped into the mind

so what does this all mean?
why are we here?
what is my purpose on this planet earth?
i mean plane

dimension?

grandfather introduced me to you when i turned 7
you showed up to my birthday party
i was oh so surprised
thought i was going to have me a friend for life

you made me laugh
you made me cry
and exposed me to new things
you entertained me like crazy
thought you were cool
took a long time to realize that you were playing me

when the other children were outside
we stayed in the house
chilling in each other's faces for hours
not realizing it was my mental you would devour

time flew by
grammar school
high school
even parts of college
we found time to enjoy each other's company
but i still didn't know that the sucking of your energy
would come for me

getting into the back of my mind
while i'm thinking everything is fine
you were part of the reason for my limited thoughts
fear
influencing behaviors
and messed up patterns in my life

how could you mess with my mind like that?
i watched programs with you
didn't know you were programming me right back

everybody raved about how good of a friend you were
they watched you and grew to love you
up in everybody's house playing cool
on the low with your subliminals
and nobody had a clue

you would gossip and tell me the latest news
but it was all scripted
it was all a lie
i used to have 20/20 vision
but befriending you made me blind

blind to what was really going on
blind to your hypnotizing effects
blind to your spells
your controlling mechanism
all of this i did not expect
everything you exposed me to was fake
our friendship
our time together
was one huge mistake

you tried to belittle me
confuse me
and even control my moods
had me receptive to your suggestions
ideas
telling me how and what to think
played me like a fool

directing and altering my mind through mental physiology
and psychological manipulation
to no longer welcome you in my home
there won't be any hesitation

i will no longer allow you to shape

and affect my perception of my reality
i will no longer allow you to seep into my subconscious
manipulate my consciousness
or allow myself to experience a mental mortality

i'd rather read a book or spend time in nature
than spend time with you
i'd rather imagine a world where you don't exist
because your presence is not beneficial to anybody
and that is the truth

you can no longer mentally abuse me
or intentionally use me
once i became aware of what you are and what you do
you started losing me

we are no longer cool
i'm throwing you out
you cannot come back into my home
i now know your purpose
i now know your agenda
i now know you're not good for my dome

i will no longer let you affect my subconscious
you will no longer get my attention

and who i'm talking about y'all

is television

i used to love h.i.m.

q. h.i.m.?

a. i got the idea of this poem when i was listening to common's song "i used to love h.e.r." i remembered the acronym was '**h**ip-hop in its **e**ssence is still **r**eal' and i figured i come up with one for my poem, and in this case h.i.m. would stand for '**h**ypnotic trance produced by television sets **i**nfluencing the **m**ind' i think that'll work (laughs).

q. so you don't watch any tv?

a. i mean here and there when i'm at other people's houses, but my own personal tv has not been turned on in over a year. as a matter of fact, it's not even plugged in and i'm still not sure as to why i haven't sold it yet (laughs). but once you truly become aware of what tv does it can't affect you much, plus you not going to want to watch too much of it anyways.

be the programmer
don’t be a victim of the programming

Kia Marlene

i take breaks

because i must recharge myself like my phone
so i isolate to be alone

i take breaks

from social media and the news
because too much will ruin you

i take breaks

from my family and my friends
introvert problems once again

i take breaks

from caring about the world's sad news and bad news
time to focus solely on my own world
no apologies if that sound rude

i take breaks

from things that's distracting
things that don't benefit me
i will be subtracting

i take breaks

to reboot
regroup
and regenerate

because i can't let society and the ways of this world have an impact on my life full time

and i can’t let unnecessary disturbances interfere with my
purpose and mission at any time

so i take breaks

to remind myself

to stay focused

sometimes we must let the darkness do its magic

Kia Marlene

i had to put the phone down
stop looking at tv
and enjoy my own company
i told distraction i will sit this one out
so don't even come for me

only entertainment i was interested in
was the reprogramming of my subconscious mind
only socializing i was doing
was with nature
the ether
and my higher self
transcending space and time

only news i cared about was from the firmament
that projected info to me on this plane
through synchronicities and signs
only media i gave my energy to
was the medium within myself
as i developed clairvoyance through my meditations
intentions
visualizations
and opening my third eye

other things became irrelevant
expanding my consciousness was relevant
becoming a grander version of myself was crucial
and necessary for my betterment

maybe changing self is helping everyone else
because i can't change the world
but i can change myself
maybe changing self is helping everyone else

because i can't change the world

but i can change myself

turn off your tv
turn off your phone
turn off your radio
and turn on your connection with your higher self

turn on your connection with the ethernet
turn on your connection with nature
all of earth and nothing else

turn off to turn on
turn off to turn on

connect

Evolution of Awareness

i had to separate from a world that was familiar
to connect with a world that became unfamiliar
i had to get rid of wi-fi, cell phones, television
and sometimes shoes because mother earth wanted me to feel her

i had to first isolate
become receptive and available to communicate
the body had to regenerate
my light was ready to further illuminate
the mind was ready to elevate
because my higher self was preparing me to build with her

i had to lose friends
but i gained wisdom
plus i was at the point
where i couldn't relate to old friends when i was with them

told myself no growth equal stagnation
self-empowered growth can bring forth new nations

so i had to become comfortable with who i was becoming
drop old ways and limited thoughts like they were nothing

i had to start talking to nature
and ask for the ear to hear nature talk back
i had to ask for a new set of eyes
in order to see things that the old set lacked

i had to become aware of the synchronicities, images and signs
become conscious of my emotions and thoughts from my mind

i had to read ancient text
stop responding to purposeless text
and prepare myself and be obtainable
for challenges and test

i know transformation may not be easy
a lot of painful wounds might rise to the surface
but i knew for the sake of unlocking my history
learning my soul and its mysteries
it will all be worth it

i had to research and realize that this universe is holographic
and that everything within is indeed without
i had to study earth
nature
epigenetics
neuroscience
parapsychology
astrology
the universal laws
and myself
to see more of what life is really about

i had to understand that everything has consciousness
and that my intention has power
i had to learn how to be present in the moment
and not worry about the next hour

i had to rediscover that all the answers i needed
were already stored within
i had to realize that god is of all things
including the gentle touch of the wind

i had to realize that in this game of life
you need to learn how to manage your energy
control your own mind
and see the bigger picture if you want to win

i had to separate from a world that was familiar

and connect with my own world within

trying to stay focused so i will lay low
about to fall back like the leaves
away from it all my conscious telling me to leave

so i will ground
hibernate
get my juice up
make room for growth

evolve some more
and bloom again
when the universe says so

because nothing else matters
even though everything is matter
trying to feed my consciousness with ancient wisdom
new beliefs and new perceptions
so that my awareness can get fatter

trying to build up my creativity
so from the field i can pull from creation
and add to it
if earth is dehydrated from low frequencies
then i will keep my vibe and thoughts high
allow them to flow like water
and add fluid

to know the secrets of my cells
no doubt i will pursue it
to figure out what's hidden in my subconscious
that can further connect me to the cosmos and my ancestors
no doubt i will get to it

because i have a new set of lens in this third dimension
because the veil has been removed
i'm just trying to stay true

stay light
and of course
stay very cool

because i'm programmed for greatness
regardless of what they try to alter
i've got certain symbols that remind me of that
i keep them by my altar

trying to decode what's been coded within my being
so i can overstand the message
curiosity and questions got my consciousness stretching
mind showing off
so it's over here flexin'

realize there's a bigger picture to see
so i'm looking at reality from a panoramic view
realized the pictured could be altered through my mind

so i allowed my thoughts to become anew

got lost in my solitude
it's pretty dark
no switch for a light
but spirit led me here
i think they're trying to show me that i am light

didn't understand it at first
but i see that they were right
didn't want to be here at first
but i chose not to put up a fight

no windows here
just my eyes cracked half way
because the soul chose not to hide
no windows here
just my eyes cracked half way
because i'm available for the soul to be my guide

the veil be the curtains
i chose to lift them up
all versions of myself through me
i choose to lift them up

my thoughts became my friends
my questions became my teachers
higher self showing me how to win at life
ancestors cheering me on from the bleachers

guides guiding me
whispers in my ear to stay strong
group hugs from invisible forces
for when the days seem long

books labeled new age containing old info
became my professors
i eventually learned to clean up my gut

became my intuitions number one investor

the exit is definitely brighter than the entrance
realized i'm a spider weaving strands on this web of existence

my awareness graduated
the soul gave out the diploma
the smell of transformation reached out to the cosmos
they rejoiced over the aroma
i once was blind
but now i see
i once was surviving
but now i be

got lost in my solitude
it's pretty dark
no switch for a light
spirit led me here
i think they're trying to show me that i am light

felt as if i didn't have my voice
but my soul spoke
each letter
each word
each line
upon each sheet of paper
my soul wrote

spotted my emotions here
they were in the lost and found

started to embrace my feelings
and also cried when i remember my mission for returning
i remembered my vow

but how could such darkness

bring this much enlightenment?
how could a shift in perception
bring this much excitement?

what was once confusion
is now clarity
what was once blurry
is now clear to me

i started a new shift
no 9-5
i started a new journey
no jeep ride

still learning because growth never stops
still learning
because

growth

never

stops

the sun shines
just for me
the birds chirp
just for me
the trees bear fruit
just for me
the ocean waves
just for me
the flowers grow
just for me
the winds blow
just for me
the butterflies fly
just for me

i am realizing that this world is functioning

just

for

me

i knew there was more to life than what i perceived
more than what i was experiencing
more than what i was aware of
and i was determined to find out what it was
and what i discovered is that
i am infinite
i am divine
i am connected to all there is

me and nature is connected
so i know the birds have a message
awakened by their melodies
i'm like, what's the news?
and i went outside to check it

they said "be receptive to our sound
stay aware of it too
"we come to bring love and light
to keep your chakras balanced and tuned"

so i began to listen
and paid close attention
it's as if the birds got louder
because they knew my intention

my intention was to be open to their healing sound
their truth and their light
to consistently experience the joy from their songs
and understand the purpose of their sight

they must have known i was conscious of them
because their chirps began to harmonize
they felt my gratitude for their existence
while their beauty kept me mesmerized

when they fly close by
i look up and say thank you
for they do so much for my being
they bring a vibe that i can't explain
and they make me smile without reason

when one of the bigger birds leave a feather for me to find
i know the angels are near
supporting and encouraging me throughout my journey
telling me "everything is fine my dear"

birds have a purpose
and is a blessing like all things on earth
i'm grateful for all that they are
and their functions
and i'm grateful for all of their work

he asked me what my favorite song was
i said it's a song that they don't play on the radio
a song that i can't download on itunes
a song that i hear live every morning
a song that makes my soul groove

it's the song that the birds sing
you know the birds outside my window
the birds that excite all of my cells
the birds that gets me off my pillow

the song with the sweetest divine harmony
the song that can never do no harm to me
the only song that does something to my existence
the only song which i can go outside and witness

the song that relaxes hearts
and soothes ears
the song that can dissolve stress
and calm fears

i don't need a tidal account or a concert ticket
i just go outside
enjoy myself
the sounds of nature

and the songs from the birds

i don't want to cut my grass anymore
i know people will say it looks wild
but what if earth's grass are antennas too?
what if the taller the grass
the greater the information that's sent through?

i like this
i think i will do this every night and day
sit in the grass barefoot
look at the sky
enjoy the moment
knowing i'm being watched by my guides

enjoy the sound of the buzzing bees
and flies in my ear as they tune me up
enjoy the vibration from earth's roots as they soothe me up

should i be more aware of my thoughts as i'm grounding?
be more observant of what surrounds me?

i feel like outside is more of my home than my actual house is
the sun is a light i don't need a switch for
the grass is a bed that, unlike the bed in my room
it can ground my conscious

the birds are my telephone
i can tell them a message
and they will send it to where it needs to go

i love this house, i love this vibe
i feel connected, i feel whole

accessing information
receiving healing and divine energy
as my soles caress the grass and become one with earth

accessing information
receiving healing and divine energy
as my soul mesh and becomes one with earth

i like this
i think i will do this every night and day
sit in the grass barefoot
look at the sky
enjoy the moment
knowing i'm being watched by my guides

i don't want to cut my grass anymore
i know people will say it looks wild

but what if earth's grass are antennas too?

butterflies
rabbits
and spiders
oh my
i keep seeing you guys in my presence
any of you want to tell me why?

are you my spirit animals?
guides?
or just signs?

do you have a message for me?
or is there anything i need to remember?
because i've been seeing you constantly
like gyms in january see new members

no but seriously
what does your presence mean?
maybe i'll just ask you guys next time i see a butterfly fly
a bunny hop
or a spider weaving its strings

whatever the case is i'm grateful that you've been sent
but please, if anybody in the cosmos can hear me
could i get a hint?

ok well maybe i'll just google it
look up the spiritual meanings of each of you
nothing is a coincidence
so there has to be a reason why i keep seeing you

butterflies
rabbits
and spiders
oh my

i even see you in my dreams at night
are you here to let me know that the ancient wisdom of my
ancestors i am in tune with?
are you guys symbols of luck?
abundance?
change?
growth?
or are you here to tell me to trust my gut
and become more intuitive?

you are placed in my world
you are placed in my sight
are you here to root for me?
tell me that i'm doing good at shining my light?

if you have a message for me
allow me to read your mind
if you are here to support and assist me
i am thankful for your guide

but seriously, are all of you my spirit animals?
if so i guess i'm lucky to have 3

butterflies
rabbits
and spiders
oh my
thank you for any lessons
gifts
wisdom

or any protection you may bring

dogs bark
birds chirp
no cars going by just stillness
sirens going off
sounds of money arriving
no illness

this is my world
so i know that these sounds are for me
so i observe with my ears
listen with my eyes
to inner-stand my reality

can i see past the micro
and comprehend the macro?
can i see past the idealizations and illusions
and make the right choices for my growth?

i continue to observe using more than just 12 senses
i greet the trees and the earth
feel the dew on the grass
stare at the sun and use all three eyes to witness

to witness what is evolving for me
to witness what is being solved for me
to witness my transformation
and the gifts that were given all to me

i take deep breaths
allowing my belly to expand
as life force fills my lungs and chest

i visualize my desires
while trying to figure out my purpose
and exhale with a thank you
for all that i will experience next

we are all magicians
and once we become aware of this
the real magic can begin

Kia Marlene

letters to my subconscious mind
unplugged clocks
because i don't care about the time

it's a full moon tonight
lunar eclipse in aquarius to be exact
fela kuti music being played
volume to the max

coconut scents from my hair
sage smoke in the air

incense lit too
beeswax candles flickering by the altar
smoke is multidimensional
let's see how reality can be stretched and altered

number 2 pencil for my sigil
ancestor pics
glass of water
a few bird feathers
crystals
rocks
and a few symbols are my visual

creating what i desire
letting go of what expired

energy and vibrations high giving it all i got
grateful for this moment and what i have
intending to receive what i request
and to let go of what i have not

lighter held to my sigil and notes
burn it up, burn it up
carbon from the lead pencil

tree from the paper i wrote

ashes move slow motion through the ether
as it returns back to earth in another form

the moon is a witness and feels it all
reacting to the intentions
shifting all waters including me
gentle breeze no storm

utilizing my power
thought is heat
i feel warm

i think the moon senses my gratitude
i should talk to her more while she lights up the night
wait
bob marley just came on

i think i'll light one tonight

12 hours around the clock
12 months
12 zodiac signs
12 planets
12 chakras
12 strands of dna
12 cranial nerves
12 universal laws
12 types of rainbows

what is it about the number 12
that i need to remember and know?
does the number 12 define and structure all that is?
how can i gain clarity about the meaning of the 12
in relation to me and the whole?
i intend to remember the purpose of 12 and its symbol
the message of 12 i will decode

12 organ systems
12 mineral cell salts
12 meridians
12 gods of olympus
12 imams
12 apostles
12 tribes
12 angels
12 crops of fruit on the tree of life
12 gates of heaven

what is it about the number 12
that i need to remember and know?
does the number 12 define and structure all that is?
how can i gain clarity about the meaning of 12
in relation to me and the whole?
i intend to remember the purpose of 12 and its symbol

the message of 12 i will decode

13 love
13 sun
but no 13 months
13 zodiac signs
13 cranial nerves
why do they keep you hidden?
13 i desire to know your biography
what do you mean to me?
me being the universe

some fear you when you fall on a friday
they call you unlucky
others love and honor you
why is the meaning of your number so diverse?

13 major joints
13 lunar cycles in a year
13th chakra being the super galactic center
but info like this we rarely hear

13
13
13

how powerful is your energy?
how deep is your mystery?
teach me your history

13th letter of the alphabet being m for man
and m for w when flipped for wombman
i'm probably going too much into detail
but 13 share with me your secrets
share with me your tales

i've changed the settings on my watch
just so i can see 13 o'clock

maybe seeing and intending to inner-stand the number 13
can activate something within me that is not

sacred
powerful
death
transformation
rebirth

i am open to your knowledge
the activation of 13 within my system
to awaken your code
to download your power
to overstand your ideology
all in the name of 13 love
just to see you work

it's information stored inside of me
that i'm determined to extract
because textbooks in schools
are not where it's at

it's time to touch the soil
and look to the sun
it's time to realize and overstand
that all is one

it's time to renovate the system
and refuse to conform to it
it's time to utilize our power
and get more informed with it

halloween is every day
because these bodies are our costumes
we are light beings and starseeds
let's finish our task
let's resume

it's time to tap into a higher consciousness
and be available for the cosmos
it's time to realize we are grand
it's time to realize what the soul knows

q. do you still believe all is one?

a. to a certain degree yes. i believe we are all a part of the one, different parts of the one, all having different experiences for the one while experiencing different states of consciousness. we are the one split up in different aspects of reality. we are all pieces of the whole and our uniqueness gives us our oneness within the one, all cut from the same cloth but connected like a quilt that has several different patches with each patch having its own special design, its own style, its own special color, and its own special pattern -- all still apart of the same blanket, all part of the same quilt. that's what i got for now, that's my theory, and i hope that wasn't too confusing (laughs). i'm still learning and processing information as i go, as i continue to inner and overstand the many pages of this book of life, as i continue to inner and overstand the many pages of my own book within this life, within this journey.

all the books in the world don't amount to the book of earth
the book of existence
the story of my cells
the tales of my soul
the passages of the sun
the narratives of the moon
the chapters of my genes
the contents of my dna
the book of me
these the books i want to read
open up
and go in
these are the pages i want to flip
time jump
and highlight
re-read and inner-stand
remember and understand
review and overstand

the book of me

is it okay that i remain true
and not restrict myself to the ways of society?
is it okay that i choose love
and to love myself entirely?
is it okay that i choose freedom
and to feel and be free within my own mind?
is it ok that i choose to view time as cyclic
and not just accept linear time?
is it okay that i walk away from what no longer serves me
and build a wall in front of those who don't deserve me?

is it okay that i choose wisdom?
wisdom of my ancestors
universal wisdom
and the wisdom of symbols?
is it okay that i choose peace
and become a stranger to fear
and a stranger to anything in the past that may have made me tremble?

is it okay that i choose nature
to teach me what instructors in a classroom can't?
is it okay that i choose the sound of the universe
practice mantras to reprogram my being
to revitalize and re-create
then proceed to chant?

is it ok that i choose the knowledge that's stored in my cells
explore the knowledge from self
instead of everyone else's information?
is it okay that i choose me
so that i can follow my own soul's journey

to experience and enjoy my own transformation?

i experience what i experience
because of my soul's desires

i am who i am
because of my soul's request

who i will be in my next lifetime
or what i will experience in my next life
will differ

because just like our desires change
the soul's desires will change as well

so i will be the best that i can be
and embrace all things with joy and gratitude

to satisfy my soul

when i made the decision to heal my soul
get to know more about my soul
and allow it to evolve
my soul heard my request

my taste buds began to transform
the kind of music i had an ear for began to change
my soul was preparing me for what was next

thoughts and images that were unusual
and felt as though they didn't belong to me
raced through my mind
but something told me that these thoughts and images
could be scenarios or experiences from a different lifetime

maybe i had to question these thoughts and images
to understand that they were telling me what the soul
experienced before me
maybe i had to forgive and embrace the undisclosed
so past experiences from my soul can become clear instead of
blurry

i realized i had to send
love
peace
and healing
to every soul that my soul was tied to
forgive myself and others
for anything unpleasant that my soul was attached to

it is my plan to heal all parts of the soul
that never received healing
tie up any loose ends of the soul
and be available for the sealing

if my soul has an open wound
i intend to be the needle and thread
that will close it up
mend and stitch it
if any parts of my soul ever been broken
i intend to manifest the tools here and now
that will make it whole again
repair and fix it

i desire to know all that my soul encountered before now
not for nothing
but to know who i am
understand my history
so that i may gain clarity of the now

i aim to grow from whatever the soul needs me to grow from
and to learn lessons from whatever the soul needs me to learn
from

i know my emotions and feelings contribute to my soul
so it is my goal to allow it to experience bliss, joy and happiness
i aspire to create divine memories
and to bring about a change within myself
i'll be my soul's activist

my soul is magnificent
divine
grand
and infinite
nothing less

my soul is all that i am now
forever evolving
forever becoming
to describe it best

i am grateful for my soul
and its communication through my being
i am excited for what we will experience next

i desired to know more about my soul
heal my soul
and allow it to evolve

my soul has heard my request

from my eyes, cob webs are leaching
my soul is doing some house cleaning

i'm no longer seeing what i'm used to seeing
no longer feeling what i'm used to feeling
who i am is doing some surface reaching
no mistake
spirit is doing some purpose teaching

lessons from my past ran laps around my experience
many opportunities to change
but i became comfortable with invariance

eventually i grew tired of the old and the same
i desired more, so a shift in consciousness was arranged

i was always light
but being aware of this i became lighter
no bleaching
i received that gospel
because through spirit my thoughts delivered the word
no preaching

my soul hungered for my attention
and to become one with oneness
is what it's beseeching
to connect and feel all areas of the web of existence
i've heard the deepest part of me loud cry for this
no screeching

intending to become available for all information
and for my evolving of awareness to remain consistent
no gaps
no breaching

intending to aim high

and never stop growing
because if transformation is at the top

i'll never stop reaching

whenever i listen to soulful afrobeat music
i began to dance like an untrained ballerina
i feel my ancestors circulating through my blood
and my living room becomes an arena

are these my dance moves, or moves from my lineage?
when vocals appear on the track
i don't know all of the words
but spirit helps me to start singing it

i sway with style and grace, flowing with ease
the only things that matter in this moment
are my vibrations and movements
all other worries and concerns are released

when those divine sounds from the instruments hit my ear
it's like the subconscious instructs me to dance
the soul says *"this sounds familiar"*
and through me the soul reminisces about a past lifetime romance

a romance for the passion
the era
the movement
and the sweet soulful sounds of afrobeat

i feel warm
i think my blood is boiling from the rhythms and tunes
my soul trying to reveal more of its history

as i twirl and move my hips throughout my arena
i remember a time that's not now
i wasn't there
but my soul was around

genetic codes in my body

got me releasing emotions over the melodies
still trying to figure out through the music
what spirit is telling me

i'm enjoying the vibes here
sweet rose incense aroma in the air
saxophones
trumpets
chanted vocals
percussion
electric guitars and drums tune up the chakras of the ear

hips slow whine in a clockwise motion
expressing my soul through dance
creating high frequency electromagnetic waves
within this cosmic ocean

these songs tell a story
i think my soul was involved in the plot
i close my eyes intending to explore my cells
while trying to remember the story
and its moral with everything i've got

as i continue to dance
beats and spirit speaking to me at the same time
the story is one that i still try and comprehend
so i keep my ancestors on the mainline

afrobeat wants me to remember the story of my own soul
as my emotions over the musical chords start to deepen
if my soul wants me to explore the pages of its book
through these tunes
then i want my mind to get deep in

all i know is that i'm enjoying the vibe
anything that needs to be revealed

i intend for it to be revealed tonight

so as i close my eyes
i visualize
that i'm jumping from concerts featuring
fela kuti
tony allen
eddie quansa
ebo taylor
chief stephen osita osadebe
and then dele sosimi performs one of my favorite songs titled
b.b.e.n.y

i appreciate the passion
i appreciate the tunes
and i appreciate the energy i feel from their music

afrobeat will always be in my heart
it will always be of my soul
it will always be in my blood

to vibe and move to it

i cannot function without music
because i am music
music i am
i am soca
calypso
zouk
kompa
dancehall
reggae
roots reggae
reggaeton
bachata
salsa
merengue
afro house
afrobeat
afro soul
i am rhythm and blues
rap
old school
new school
hip hop
punk rock
classic, modern and traditional pop
i am the blues
jump blues
blue grass
jazz
soul jazz
vocal jazz
jazz fusion
jazz funk
acid jazz
free jazz
easy listening
drum and bass

swing
electro swing
new jack swing
i am disco
oldies but goodies
classical
acoustic
funk
neuro funk
liquid funk
bebop
a human beat box
rock&roll
roll&rock
i am country
ragtime
deep house
soulful house
house music
jungle music
techno
dub
dubstep
rocksteady
steady i rock
i am negro spirituals
christian hymns
gospel
i am the gospel
the truth
and the truth is
i cannot function without music
because i am music

music i am

when life gets confusing
put on your favorite tune
and just dance

Kia Marlene

put on your favorite tune
dance til your soul fills up the room
dance til you emit waves of flowers waiting to bloom
dance til you feel the rhythm rise up your spine, energizing your chakras and your mood
dance like it's the longest day of the year (*the 21st of June)*
dance til your red blood turns to blue
dance til the sun shines its brightest
and changes your day to joy, from gloom
dance til the day goes dark and it's just you and the moon
dance til you feel the ether join in and vibe with your grooves
dance til your body becomes the melody, as your mind wander and get loose
dance til you become sound and no longer hear sound

but only the voice of spirit speaking through

dance

q. dance til your soul fills up the room?

a. yup, why not, right? (laughs). i definitely remembered what triggered this poem. i had just got finished dancing and listening to hector lavoe's "aguanile" and as many times as i've heard that song, something on that day told me to get up and dance. i literally felt spirit taking over. i felt like i was no longer here. it's like i travelled somewhere else in that moment and experienced more than just the song and my dance moves. i guess sometimes dancing will do that; spirit within will get loose, come out and take you with it. i felt like i was floating right before i actually came back down. i felt good, i felt liberated, i felt awakened.

listening to childish gambino album "awaken, my love!"
had me reminiscing about when my higher self grabbed my
attention and said *"awaken my love"*

since then i stayed woke
learned how to manage my energy
and paid full attention to my awareness

researched quantum physics
the 12 universal laws
discovered more about parallel universes
because all of this knowledge i had an eye and ear for this

if you would've asked me if i was woke 3 years ago
i would've replied yes because i saw hidden colors 1-4
ask me today and i'll say yes because i got introduced to ramtha
the pleiadians and the information within me that was already
stored

but that goes to show that evolution is a process
yes i'm awake to what i'm available for
but what i'm not yet open to the mind can't process

i intend to be open for what's necessary
and imperative for my growth
i intend to remind myself
that i am connected to an existence

that may be grander than what i currently know

i remember at one point
i used to try to fit in so much
that i wasn't even sure if i was being myself

Kia Marlene

i remember when i used to live for others
i remember when i used to live for society
i remember when my fire didn't spark
and nothing was igniting me

i remember when the ego was on top
and the soul was left behind
i remember when i cared what others thought
and didn't think with my own mind

i remember when i let the media tell me how to dress
and how to wear my hair
i remember when i used to think life was happening to me
and none of it was fair

i remember when i thought i was alone
and no one heard me
i remember when self-love was non-existent
and i allowed others to hurt me

i remember when i did what others wanted me to
instead of doing for self
i remember when i valued material things
more than my own health

i remember when i allowed distractions
to obscure the voice within
i remember when my thoughts were negative
and i allowed fear and doubt to win

i remember when i had no vision
no motivation
and no goals
i remember not realizing that life was responding to me
and i kept my vibrations low

i remember when i didn't learn from life lessons
and kept repeating them
which inhibited my growth
i remember when i felt lost
although on the right road

i remember when i used to be glued to the television
not realizing i was being programmed
because the subconscious run this
i remember when i thought i was separate from all there is
and wasn't conscious of my oneness

i remember the night spirit awakened me
and whispered in my ear saying
we need you now

i remember all of these things
i have no regrets
because it has led me to where i am now

strong

powerful

and evolving

silence the music of the world
and tune into the song your heart plays

Kia Marlene

i intend to silence the outside world
and listen to the world of my own
i intend to acknowledge all consciousness
as they are aware of me when i roam

seems like the more 528hz music i listen to
the more emotional i become
is it because love is overpowering my being
allowing me to realize all is one?

they say the body is held together by sound
is that why we have 12 organs?
is that why everything is a vibe
and being cautious of what we're near
and what we hear is important?

i intend to silence the outside world

and listen to the world of my own

i stopped listening to the message
about worshipping a messenger
that was outside of me
and started listening to the message within

Kia Marlene

she was searching for god
and found herself, she said
she searched high and low
near and far
and realized god can't be identified outside of who we are

this force that's within us
is the force that makes you, *you*
this force is the force which we create
and evolve through

but even with all this information ingestion
on this journey she still had questions

"if we are made in god's image
am i god's clone?
god's duplicate?

am i an extension of god exploring this field of existence
and am i here to add to it?

does the real trinity have a different meaning
than what they teach?
let's say god is the husband
the soul is the wife
and the son is me?

or is the trinity our minds
because you know we have three

is god the unconscious mind?
the soul the subconscious mind?
and the conscious mind the ego?

if all things are intertwined and connected
then there is only one and no trio?

father?
son?
holy spirit?

proton?
neutron?
electron?

god is light, right?
so is god a photon?

i know my body is the temple of god
and the spirit of god dwells in me
and because of these facts i know i am divinity

but yet i still wonder
am i just a thought in god's mind?
no seriously, is my being just a thought in god's mind?

is god imagining?
was i manifested because god loved the thought of me as a
character in this dream world?
or is god communicating through my emotions?
the emotions that connect me to the spirit world?

if god became man so that man may become god
am i in training to become the god that is of me?
do i have to live
and experience every form of life throughout time?
grow
mature
and evolve until i become the god that is within me?

if god is the creator
then am i a co-creator?

if i am the illustration
is god the illustrator?"

all of these questions made a trail
a trail back to herself
a trail back to the realization that she is evolving beautifully
with the assistance from her higher self

she searched high and low
near and far
but realized god can't be identified outside of who we are
she said

she was searching for god

and found herself

she said

a poem about god?
okay, let me see how i can do this
should i just grab the pen
don't think
just write
and let the soul do this?

i'm still trying to figure it all out myself
i think my guides knew this
but i gathered a lot of information from within and without
so let me try to infuse this

when i hear or see the word god
i don't think of a man living in the sky
at a time i did
but now when i think of god
i think of you and i

god is the essence of all that exists
god is pure energy
god is the voice in my mind
god is the inner me

when i realized this
i saw the whole world differently
when i gained understanding
i began to live life more efficiently

i began to realize that god is not just one person
but within all persons
i began to realize that god is not just one thing
but of all things

i remembered that god is within me
working behind the seen
the unseen

and being the seen

i remembered that god is within me
working behind the scenes
on the scene
and being the scene

god is love
so love all that you see
for all that you see is you

god is the environment
god is nature
the multiverse
and the stars too

god is all thoughts
god is emotion
god is your most innermost feelings

god is the voice that clings to your soul
be still and listen to what it's revealing

god is consciousness
your awareness
god simply just is

god is forever creating
forever evolving
god is all of this

god is infinite
without beginning
and indeed
without end

god is all knowingness
light and dark
prime creator
and infinite intelligence

god is the teacher
god is the student
god is the whole entire school

god is the raindrops
the wave
the ocean
and the dew

god is inexpressible
a high frequency
the essence that gives life to all

god is in all things
god is of all things

gaining experience from it all

one day i decided i was done

i was done with the leave-ins and the shampoos
i was done with the twisting of the hair
and the oiling of the scalp
i was done with the deep conditioners and the combs
i was done with hot oil treatments and the clipping of the ends
i was done with preventing my hair from being intelligent

i was done with the creams
i was done with the grease

i was done with not allowing my hair to just be

if we are designed to be far greater
than any computer that can be created
then isn't the hair that's attached to my being far greater
without the need to be manipulated?

water
love
and sunlight is all that it needs

so anything other than that

i decided i was done

q. no shampoos? no oiling of the scalp? no grease?

a. (laughs) okay okay okay, maybe natural shampoo here and there and a little castor oil or mustard oil when i think of it (laughs), but nothing too much. i'm realizing i love simplicity and since i stopped doing so much to my hair it's become the healthiest it's ever been. just like our bodies are intelligent and always making its way towards health, if we treat it naturally, our hair does the same thing.

dear human body i praise you and i cherish you
i am extremely grateful for all that you are capable of
your divine shield and unique build
all of it i indeed love

you are amazing and magnificent
all that you are i have yet to learn
all that you possess and able to do
to experience it i indeed yearn

i am grateful for the things you do for me
without me even knowing
i am grateful for every part of you
even the parts that are not showing

you are powerful
you are grand
you are beautiful to my eye
but this is your eye
you house me
for i am light in disguise

you're so special
the totality of you is holographic
i can heal you with my mind
no meds needed
no surgeries
nope, nothing drastic

they taught me that you and the mind are not one
and that you are separate from my thoughts
but that is indeed false

the outcome of your health is the effect
my thoughts are the cause

the mind can heal scars on your skin
no bandage no gauze
my mind can heal any scars within
no therapist no cost

i embrace and take full responsibility
for any expression that you express
i am grateful to experience you during the tough times of pain
and during the times i feel my best

you are the vehicle
my mind is the driver behind the wheel
i'm steering for greatness
gliding effortlessly up every hill

because, to the top, we got to make it
divine health
strength
inner peace
balance and harmony
you name it

superb energy
love
flexibility of the mind and body
i will definitely claim it

even after future decades to come
the greatest scientist still won't be able to understand your machinery
all that you are and do for me
not sure if you know how much you mean to me

you are forever transforming
within and without
you are never sick

you just release what the mind didn't make peace with
or let out

everything happens through you
so it explains why you must react
physical cleanse
mental cleanse
even the thoughts the mind attract

the fact that you and the mind are one
i won't think light of it
you were working for me
before i was even conscious of it

now that i know
i will take care of you naturally
and my thoughts will remain positive
if i experience anything that's not pleasing
then i will assume that i am the cause of it

you store life
spirit
divine energy
and i am grateful for the housing
i intend to keep us feeling good

and of course looking astounding

this is the part where i have to tell you
i choose me
this is the part where i have to tell you
we can no longer be

this is the part where i have to tell you
i no longer want to participate in the sexual exchange of energy
this is the part where i have to tell you
there was never really any chemistry

this is the part where i have to tell you
"no, i won't come through"
and that i will no longer allow my body to be a playground for your pleasure

this is the part where i have to tell you
my awareness has changed
i'm not the same
and i am conscious of the consciousness of my body
and my body i will now treasure

this is the part where i have to tell you
and the flawless sculpture of your physique
goodbye

this is the part where
love for me
love for my body
rise and comes alive

so long

i can't have sex with you
because i'd rather be deeply in love with you
before i share my body
i can't allow my soul to tie with just anybody

you don't love me
and i don't love you
sex is more than an exchange of pleasure
it's an exchange of information too

i love and value myself
do you love and value you?
because intertwining with insecurity
and lack of self-love
i can't do

do you have resentment in your heart
or hidden anger that don't show?
i can't have that type of energy mixing with my spirit
leaving imprints on my soul

should i allow your sex to stimulate my chakras
open and align them with the energy you embody?
if i can't feel you without feeling you
then should i let your energy enter my body?

should i allow you to come into my sacred space
and explore all that's divine?
do i want to activate kundalini energy with you
and allow it rise up my spine?

do i truly know you?
what are your thoughts and intentions like?
do you vibrate high?
do you care for your body right?

should i share my orgasmic experience with you
while i'm able to travel to other dimensions?
or share my magic with you?
since sexual energy can manifest one's desires
info i must mention

i can't have sex with you until i can trust you
until i can love you
until i know that my mind and soul has touched you

until i can feel you penetrate my soul
before i allow you to penetrate my body
until i know that you adore just me
and not loving everybody

until i know for a fact that i'm the only one you're thinking of

plus, i can't have sex with you

because i prefer to make love

yoni steam
sage smoke
candle light
my thoughts
and intending to heal and let go of what's not peace, love and
balance is what i write

dear yoni
how dare i love myself so much that i would allow something
not of love to enter my internal space?
putting my physical needs first
and allowing love to be in last place?

how dare i not allow tender, love and care *tlc*
yet i allow meaningless whispers from others
to penetrate each ear
creating red light specials
tlc

being available for pleasure
but not love to enter my sacred site?
sacrificing the love for myself
to satisfy another just for one night?

focusing on my wants
and forgetting about your needs?
saying "i'm doing this for us"
when i was really doing it for me

not being in tune to your signals and your warnings?
resulting in feelings of regret during some nights
and some mornings

not realizing you want
what i truly deserve
a feeling of love

a feeling of worth

forgive me for the times you cried out
where i wasn't conscious of your tears
forgive me for anytime you felt violated
and i wasn't aware

to love me is to love you
and to only allow love to come through
to love me is to love you
and to only allow love to come through

so if sex extends deep to cellular levels
and produces an energy that can create stronger energy fields
let's create one of love
if sex is a ritual grander than what i'm currently aware of
then i want the ritual to at least be one of love

accept my apology for the times i ignored you
and ignored what you deserve
accept my apology for the times i allowed draining energy to
enter your walls
and you, i did not preserve

it is my intention to make peace with you
heal with you
to cherish and inner-stand you
to respect you
to honor you
and to always show love to you

if i've ever unintentionally put you in situations where you felt
uncomfortable
it is my bad
from this day forward you will only experience love from me
love from another

to match the love that you are
and the love from me you should've had

so i'm no longer giving tours of my sacred site
unless they come with a pass of love
other than that it just won't feel right

i'm no longer engaging in sexual activity
if love is absent
then my yoni won't be present
we will hibernate
so we can heal right

so when it comes to making love
i won't act with my mind
i will intuitively feel and act through my womb

i love me
i love us

so yoni

this is for you

when people tell me that i’ve lost weight
i don’t take it as them saying i was once fat
and now i’m slim and not curvy

i take it as i’ve mentally shed off what no longer serves me
i take it as i’ve mentally shed off what no longer deserves me

didn’t have to physically workout
but when i said i wanted to let go of the unnecessary
i’m led to believe that spirit heard me

didn’t have to physically stretch my body
instead i stretched my consciousness
to create a new version of me

exercised my mind within the cosmic sea

rose up

and experienced the emergence of me

you are the paint brush
the paint
and the portrait
create what thou wish to experience

Kia Marlene

she didn’t realize she was the ocean
and not just a wave
or that time is not what it seems
and there’s no such thing as counting the days

she didn’t realize she was grand
and a part of the whole
or that all is one
stemming from one soul

she didn’t realize that the true temple is her body
and that her body is her mind
or that she was divinely guided
and provided for with signs

she didn’t realize that the past is not the past
and that the future already exist
or that she could connect with her higher self
and ask for her assist

she didn’t realize that if she changed her thoughts
she can change her experiences
or that if she changed her perceptions
she could let go of old views she was carrying

she didn’t realize that she had 5 other chakras
outside the 7 that she knew of
or that information is stored deep inside her
and that when going within
she would receive assistance from above

she didn’t realize that consciousness
is indeed in all things
or that there were many other universes
and many other realities

she didn't realize that there was a connection
between science and spirituality
or that by forgetting her oneness to all
she was creating an illusionary duality

she didn't realize that she was an extension of the creator
a co-creator gathering information
and sending it back to the source
or that she is love
love being the most powerful force

she didn't realize that the extent of her growth
also affected the planets' growth
or that she had the ability to manifest things
by changing her beliefs and her ways of thinking
so she started doing both

she didn't realize that this may not have been her first time here
on this planet called earth
or how important she is to the vast
she didn't know her worth

she didn't realize that there were other states of consciousness
for her to explore
or that by just changing her attitude and being positive
her own health could be restored

she didn't realize that her emotions connected her
with her spiritual self
which exists within the multidimensional sphere
or that she had the power to create reality through her will
once she put an end to all fear

she didn't realize all of these things
because she forgot what she once knew
but once she remembered all of this

it's as though her life was made anew

i'm grateful for
the setbacks
the nights i cried
the times of confusion
when i didn't understand why

the isolation from the world
the hibernation
the guidance i received
during a certain situation

the so-called tough times
the universe was just showing me my strength
the life lessons i encountered
although then i knew not what they meant

the enlightenment
the growth
the awakening of my power

and the light i have now

which was discovered

during my darkest hour

q. so the dark wasn't bad after all?

a. no, not at all. a lot of lessons were learned and a lot of transformation took place. i've realized that the dark is not really dark, it's our perception of it, it's how we go through it-- nothing is never what it seems. i've learned to embrace it all, and instead of questioning "why me," i now ask "what is needed of me, how can i be of service and available for what is taking place, how can i assist the assistance that is assisting me as i continue to grow, learn and move forward on this journey." transformation will always happen, transformation will continue to take place, even beyond chapter 2, even beyond this book, and i will continue to write about it. i will continue to embrace it all.

q. what else did you write about while on this journey?

a. i wrote about heartbreak and love.

q. interesting, i wouldn't have expected that in this book. what made you write about heartbreak and love?

a. well, heartbreak and love are a part of the journey, i don't know too many people who can say they never been in love, fell out of love, or had their heart broken. those experiences alone all helps us to evolve in one way or another. plus a chapter all about heartbreak and love gives us a little break from all the deep poems (laughs).

q. so have you ever been in love?

a. maybe.

q. well, have you ever had your heart broken?

a. maybe.

q. maybe?

a. yes, maybe (laughs).

it's funny how
i want to write a poem
about you
but the stanzas fail
to appear on these lines

like how your love for me failed to appear in my life

Intermission
(heartbreak&love)

you came into my world
made me develop feelings for you
and then you left
you left as though my feelings would leave as quickly as you

and i sort of wish they did

why does it feel like my heart is broken
before we even fell in love
why does this relationship feel like it's over
before it even started
why does this feel like a goodbye
before an official hello

why does this feel like something that i've felt before

i think everything i hear and see reminds me of you
because our internal world
is our external world
and i can't seem to get you out of my mind

i sometimes wish i could

he said “why would you want to get me out of your mind?”

because i’m unsure if i’m still in yours

i'm feeling like el debarge
because i want to sing to you
and tell you that
all this love is waiting for you
but in the same breath
i want to tell you that this love won't wait forever

i waited

i waited for your heart to express itself
i waited for your actions to reveal to me
what your mouth wouldn't confess
i waited for your soul to recognize me as home
i waited for you to desire eternity with me
i waited for our beginning to begin

i waited

and i waited

until i realized i got stood up

i got stood up by your love

it never showed

your love for me

never showed

i stopped waiting for that train that may never come
that ship that may never sail
that bus that may never pull up to my stop
that text that may never be sent
that call that may never be dialed
or the words i wanted to hear come out of your mouth

i stopped waiting
i stopped waiting

i stopped waiting for you to make my vision of us real
for you to complete my world
for you to make my ever after happily
and officially make me your girl

i stopped waiting
i stopped waiting

i stopped waiting on you
because somebody may be waiting on me
i stopped waiting on you
because somebody

may be waiting on me

sometimes
i break my own heart
by falling too soon

especially when i'm the only one falling

it was fun
until i realized
that i was the only one who caught feelings

Kia Marlene

i had a whole conversation in my head with you
before i actually picked up the phone

i'm frightened that i will never be able to express myself to you
i'm frightened that you may not feel the same way
i'm frightened that you might not want me
the way that i want you
and catching feelings for you was a mistake

i told you i loved you a million times in my mind
but i can't even began to whisper it into your ear
i can't even began to tell you that i want more
more of you near

i wish you could feel me
but you don't
i wish you could express something
that will make me feel less crazy
but you wont

i wish we shared the same feelings
but i only feel as though i'm alone

i had a whole conversation in my head with you

before i actually picked up the phone

i fell
you watched me fall
and didn't fall with me
you watched me fall
and didn't fall with me

i fell

for you

i just wished we could've fallen together

your heart plays my favorite song
it's the only song i play on repeat
it's the only song i listen to
since you're no longer here with me

i memorized the tone
beat and melody
still mesmerized by the vibes you used to give to me
still wishing i can do more than imagine you near to me
still hoping you'll realize you need to be here with me

as my mind and ears replayed this tune of you
my tears came out to put on a show
they danced slow motion
and my face became their stage

your energy became trapped within my aura
that even if it was negative
i wouldn't be able to clear it with the strongest sage

i'm hooked on you
but you barely feel me
all of me screams your name
but you barely hear me

i sometimes wish you would feel the same as i
i sometimes wish these tears wouldn't flow from my eye

your heart plays my favorite song
it's the only song i play on repeat
i just wish i could hear it live

so that my soul would feel complete

i didn’t sign up for heartbreak
i signed up for love
but somehow i received both
you loved my heart

and then you broke it

nothing numbs this pain

not alcohol
or mary jane

my heart is broke

i felt the very moment it cracked

i felt all of its pieces shatter
i felt my heart drop from out of my chest
i witnessed my heart cry
i mopped up the tears with garments he left

i felt my heart let go of life
i felt my heart let go of love

i just want my heart back

but she doesn't trust me anymore
she doesn't trust my choices in men

i became heartless

he broke it

she left

i did not protect her
i thought that was the man's job to do
to protect my heart

but he left
and so did she

i'm alone

nothing numbs this pain

i typed a long message
that i was going to send to you
but then i backspaced all the way back
until i couldn't backspace no more
and then i closed the whole message away
because i realized that it doesn't matter

because i know you don't care

so now i'm asking the same question as lisa fischer
"how can i ease the pain?"
well the only time i don't feel it is when i'm laughing
so i guess i'll search for a comedy club that's open 24/7
pack a few things
grab a pillow
and see if i can move in
because i don't want to feel this pain anymore
and right now laughter is the only thing that eases it

i just hope the comedians are good

my tears are keeping me company
since you're no longer here with me
my tears hugged my cheeks
and that was the only affection that i felt
my tears are my friends tonight
as love songs bring them out of hibernation
my tears left a message on my face
i went to look in the mirror
and the message read
you will be fine
you, my friend

will be fine

i wish i could close my eyes and make the pain disappear
i wish my heart didn't have to suffer
i wish you actually cared

i wish this heartbreak was an illusion
but these wounds are real
i wish i could just move forward
so that these wounds can heal

don't know if i should be mad at you for breaking my heart
or yearn for you to repair it and make it whole
don't know if i should be strong and adjust to a life without you
or try to give us another go

all i know is that a healed heart is the goal
whether i achieve that with you or alone

but right now my feelings is hurt
and i can't stop these tears

i wish i could close my eyes

and make the pain disappear

i peeled back layers of myself
to get to my heart
just so i can offer it to you
and you declined

you declined my love

as if it were a phone call you were trying to avoid

you are like a magazine that i subconsciously subscribed to
i wish i can cancel you
but every time i try to forget about your existence
thoughts of you become renewed every month

i felt like i've read all of the articles of your mind
but i still can't seem to find anything about me
i felt like i've allowed you to pile up in areas of my heart
and it's looking like it's time that i set you free

i wish i can dust off all of these thoughts of you
box them up
and let them sit outside of my mind

i wish i can dust off all of these thoughts of you
box them up
and leave them behind

it's time i unsubscribe from your mailing list
care less about your articles
since you don't see me in your world the way i see you in mine

it's time that i cancel you all together

and move forward with my life

i've given up on love
i quit
and no
i didn't put in my two weeks notice
why should i be working for love

when love is not working for me?

now i'm feeling like carl thomas
because i wish i never met him

i wish i never

fell in love with the magical stories his eyes told
got attached to the energy his spirit holds
melted over the sound of his deep vocal tone
considered his very own heart my home
enjoyed the way he licked his lips
liked the way he tasted my kiss
allowed his smile to make me blush
wasted time daydreaming of us
found small humor in his simple jokes
felt enchanted from the words he spoke
fell for his mentality and his charm
felt safe around his presence and under his arms
had high hopes for our future and togetherness
invested my energy to visualize our foreverness
heard my heart beat from thoughts of him
drowned in my feelings where i could no longer swim

i wish i could've dodged this whole entire experience
i wish i never met him

his soul unscrewed the hinges from my guard
it got let down
i got too attached
he got too close

and i wish i never let him

how could you not miss me?

did our conversations mean anything?
did my presence not leave an impact?
did the meeting of our souls not leave and imprint?
didn't my love for you impress parts of your subconscious?

how could you not miss me?

and if you do, how could you let the tug of war
between logic and emotion
left brain and right brain
masculine and feminine
disrupt what your heart wants to show?

how could you not miss me?

i gave you pieces of me that i didn't know i had
i gave you attention before i gave it to myself
i gave you love that i kept hidden
and didn't show to anyone else

how could you not miss me?

i could've sworn i left half of my heart inside of yours
i could've sworn i left parts of my essence
wandering through your veins
i could've sworn on my soul's contract
that we both signed our names

how could you not miss me?

how could your awareness be so impaired from society
and this physical world
that you cannot see it is me you chose
before you even chose this life

how could you ignore the beating of your heart
when it tells you to reach out
but instead you choose not to

how could you not miss me?

how could you fight a fight that you know you'll lose
the fight in realizing you love me so much that it scares you
and you pull away
you pull away from experiencing a love that's out of this
dimension and you choose to settle for a love that's trapped in
the third

how could you not miss me?

i am not your soul mate
your twin flame
or your lover
i am the other half of your heart in human form
so i ask

how could you not miss me?

i feel deeply and sometimes i wish there was a
switch for that…
so i can turn it off when i want

Kia Marlene

does anybody know where the switch is?
the switch to turn these feelings off
because i'm tired of feeling so deeply

i'm tired of wearing my heart on my sleeve
with a sign that reads *warning: i may love hard*
and i'm tired of those that come into my life
experience my love
and leave
because, for them, it's too much
so they make it difficult for me to even want to love hard

i'm tired of my heart catching the holy ghost
for souls that visit this temple without intending to stay
i'm tired of my heart acting as a home
for those who treat it like a shelter
and eventually go astray

i don't want to feel no more
at least, not so much
for once i just want to feel
when i feel the feeling is mutual
for once i just want to feel

when i feel the feeling is mutual

i'm over it
i'm over you
i'm over us
i'm over thoughts of us
i'm over thinking that we will be more than what we are now
(whatever that is)
i'm over thinking that you would actually want more
(because i did)
i wanted more

but now i'm over it

i'm done picturing us together
when the frame is nonexistent
i'm done showing you my heart
when your love is not a witness

i'm done thinking that one day we could actually be

everything you are
is everything somebody wants
don’t change
just be

Kia Marlene

i may not be your cup of tea
but i'm someone's liter of fresh pressed juice
i may not be your sun
but i'm someone's full moon
i may not be the apple of your eye
but i'm the pomegranate of another's
i may not be your snack
but i'm someone's supper
i may not be your honey dip
but i'm someone's sugar cane
i may not be your shot of whisky
but i'm someone's mary jane
i may not be your rose
but i'm someone's blue lotus
i may not be your flame
but i'm someone's explosive
i may not be your world
but i'm someone's multiverse
i may not be your favorite song
but i'm someone's favorite verse
i may not be your shining star
but i'm someone's constellation
i may not be the energy you want
but i'm someone's highest vibration
i may not be your bridge over troubled water
but i'm someone's rescue boat
i may not be your better half
but i'm someone's whole
i may not be your ride or die
but i'm someone's ride and ascend
i may not be your favorite thought
but i'm someone's manifestation and win

i'm something to someone

it's funny how a certain song can come on
and make me think about you
bring up old memories
from out of the blue

bring up these feelings
that i thought were through
bring up these emotions
where past thoughts become new

so i replay this certain song
to reminisce about the way i used to feel
i smile and think of what could've been
until i realize that what could've been is not

so i let the track finish
and choose not to press replay
i let the track finish
and choose to move forward to the next song

i myself

also move forward

i've already written too much about him
these poems are not bringing him back
his chapter is done
so these pages i will rip and discard

just like he did my heart

i refuse to write any more words about you

the last stanza was about you
the last poem was about you
my last lifetime was about you

so i refuse to write anymore words
and let them be about you

you already consume most of my thoughts

i can't let you consume most of my art as well

i can finally listen to love songs without thinking about you

i can finally listen to my anita baker pandora station
without crying after every other song
i can finally listen to the quiet storm
without feeling a storm raging in my heart

i can finally listen to love songs
without thinking there's no more hope for me
i can finally listen to love songs
and smile about how perfect my future love life will be

because i know i deserve the kind of love
that the children read about in fairytales
the kind of love that's not shallow nor fake
but a love that's deep and truly real

so when i listen to love songs
i will no longer think about the love i thought i had
i will now only think about the love i know i'll have

because if the love we receive
is based on the love we give ourselves
then i know i am worthy of a love that will hug my soul
like nothing else

so the next love song i hear
i will not feel sad or blue
i will imagine that i'm singing that love song
to the true love of my life
and i will be glad that i can finally listen to love songs

without thinking about you

the day i stop writing poetry about you
is the day
that i'll know
i've moved on

Kia Marlene

my heart has been broke
my feelings have been hurt
my expectations have been crushed
so why should i give anyone a chance anymore?

why?

because they'll say they're not like the others?
well that's what the others said

so i refuse to get attached
i refuse to love hard
i refuse to get my hopes up
just to be let down
i refuse to feel for anyone who doesn't feel for me

i will no longer expose my heart
i will no longer expose my feelings
i will no longer expose my love
until real love is being exposed to me

because i'm sick of these imitations

these imitations of love

they say love isn’t supposed to hurt.
i guess i haven’t experienced real love yet

Kia Marlene

i don't know how to get attached to anyone anymore
it's like i was born with an adhesive strip on my heart and
affixed myself to everything i thought was love
but when i realized that what i thought was love
was something else
i grew tired of bonding with an imitation that couldn't live up to
the original

so i ripped the adhesive strip from off of my heart
placed it on some wood chips
and poured over it the tears i collected from over the years
from heartbreaks which i stored in mason jars that eventually
fermented and became flammable

i struck a match
greeted the flames
watched my attachment burn slowly
as i smiled at the thought of no more pain
and from me no longer allowing anyone to express to me
an imitation of love

so not only do i not know how
but i'm probably unable get attached to anyone anymore

so if a guy comes along
and try to show me what real love is
i just hope he loves me
more than i ever loved anyone before him
i hope he loves me more than i love myself
(if that's even possible)
i hope he loves me so much that love itself will give me a call
and say *hey, let this one in*

because if his existence doesn't make my soul feel like a cup of
dairy free hot chocolate while wearing thick thermal socks
cuddled up in a snuggie blanket
on a cold winter night in buffalo new york
then i can't let him in
and if his soul doesn't urge my heart
to manifest a new adhesive strip
so that our 4th chakras can mesh and stick
then i can't get attached
and i can't let him in if his effort
and the desire to have a life with me is not a match

because i don't know how to get attached to anyone anymore
the few that i did get attached to took the sticky parts
from the adhesive strip on my heart when they left
so i ripped off my attachment, which was no longer sticky
or attachable and burned what was left

so if anybody get attached to me
and wants the same in return
i really hope they're good at magic
because i don't know how to get attached to anyone anymore
my heart no longer sticks

i no longer stay

he asked me to wait for him
i replied "i'm sorry, i can't do that"
nothing against you
it's just that there were a few before you
that asked me to do that very same thing
you know...
wait
and i got tired of waiting for something to happen
i got tired of waiting for nothing to happen
so i'm sorry if i can't be like whitney houston
and tell you that i will save all my love for you
you either have it now or not at all
so no
i won't wait
i'm all out of waits
and i won't restock none for you
i deserve someone who won't ask me to wait

and apparently that's not you

the universe sends me these guys
and i think to myself
which one is my soulmate in disguise?

all the others fell through
and to make it work, i tried
but it's getting kind of old now
not having someone by my side

so i ask
does a soulmate even exist for me?
if so
does he yearn for me?
to look for me does he try?

i'm tired of dealing with souls
that aren't meant to pair with mine
i'm tired of entertaining hearts
that don't entertain mine

i wonder if there will ever be a ribbon for our love in the sky?
you know, like that stevie wonder song
but to question if a soulmate even exist for me
am i wrong?

because i'm ready for good morning texts
to turn into good morning kisses
i'm ready for the term bae
to turn into the term mrs

i'm ready for a love that is promising
a love that is favorable
a love that is propitious
i'm ready for a love that will feed and nourish my soul
a love that is nutritious

but still i ask
does a soulmate even exist for me?
if so
does he yearn for me?
to look for me

does he try?

empty thoughts and a half-filled heart
waiting for you so that our love can be birthed

waiting for you to give me thoughts of us
waiting for your love to give me a reason to blush
waiting for you so my heart can open its doors
waiting for your energy so i can feel you through my pores

i think i saw you the other day
did you see me?
i think i felt you the other day
did you feel me?

i know i've come across your path
i'm just not sure which avatar you chose this time around
i know i've heard you in my sleep
i'm just not sure if i can recall the sound

see i loved you before i was even able to pronounce the word
love, i loved you before my return here was announced from
above

i just wish i could remember
what year we had planned to meet in
on this plane called earth
i just wish i knew if we were close
or at least on the same turf

empty thoughts
and a half-filled heart
waiting for you

so that our love can be birthed

i can't tell you why the caged bird sings
but i can tell you why my caged heart bleeds

it bleeds because it is dying for a love that it has not yet experienced
it yearns for a love that may not exist
it's tired of sending out love and not feeling it back
so instead
it feels dismissed

my heart bleeds
it leaks
because no other heart has come to seal the whole
my heart bleeds
it leaks
because no other heart has come to refill it
no one has come to make it whole

yes, i love me more than newborns love their mother
but life is about balance
and it's time i experience love from another

it's time my heart experience love from not just me
but from a mate
a partner
a twin flame
or a lover
my heart has a talent in loving without limits
it's time for my heart to be discovered

my heart is caged
and locked
because i haven't met no one who has the key to free it like meek
my heart is caged
and locked

because i haven't met no one who wants to love it as much as i
love me

so i can't tell you why the caged bird sings
but i can tell you why my caged heart bleeds

it bleeds because it is losing life

from not feeling love from another being

i already fell in love with myself
i'm ready to be with somebody
who can do the same

fall in love with me

how i did

i'm tired of believing that everyone i meet is my soulmate
i'm tired of believing in love at 1st text

i'm tired of believing that i will fall in love with my instagram
crush
i'm tired of daydreaming about who i will meet next

i decided to change gears
not care
and to let things flow

i am love

so true love

will eventually

have to show

one day
when the one that is meant for me
finally shows up in my world
i will look back
and laugh
at all the other worlds i thought i was supposed to be in
and he will show me that i belong in his
and his world will feel like home

and my world will be complete

just when i thought i was finished
love gave me another reason to write
and when i thought it wouldn't happened

it did

i'm in love
with the thought
of loving him

Kia Marlene

i want to say what i wish to say
but i don't know how

i want to feel how i wish to feel
but i tell myself not now

i want to express what i wish to express
i want to scream it out loud

i want to be on a stage
unzip my ego
be bare with my soul

with you

only you in the crowd

i don't care if i feel as though i love you already
and i barely even know you
loving you raises my vibration
so i will love you in my mind

until i can love you in this life

it’s like you found me
around the same time that *i* found me

Kia Marlene

i get high off your likes

i don't care about anybody else's
because when i get notified that you've liked one of my photos
it's like i received a hit just from you hitting that heart symbol
it's like your energy double taps into my veins
once i see that you have double tapped onto one of my photos

because i get high off your likes

i get high from seeing your name listed in my notifications
i get high every time i see that number 1 red circle
in the upper right hand corner
and i see that it's from you
i get high because i'm an addict for your likes
i'm an addict for the words that you type and send to me
i'm an addict for knowing that you've viewed all of my
instagram story

because i get high off your likes

i get high from the exchange of our dm's
i get high from just thinking that
one day i may actually meet him
last time i felt this way about another in the back of my mind
i knew things wouldn't materialize
but with you
it's a different kind of vibe

it's like you found me around the same time that *i* found me
so is it possible for an instagram crush
to turn into computer love
which may turn into real love in real life?

i don't care if i sound crazy
feel deeply

overthink and overanalyze
all i know is that you touching that heart symbol
sending that dm
or viewing my instagram story
raises my vibe

because i get high off your likes

i get high every time you post
i get high from the love towards me you show
i'm an addict for your virtual energy
because baby

i get high

off your likes

i wish we could do more than exchange dm's

i wish we could exchange numbers

then exchange texts
then dialogue over the phone
then in person next
i wish we could exchange kisses

then exchange affection
exchange a passionate romance
without egos disrupting the session

i wish we could exchange sexual energy

exchange lust
exchange love

exchange trust

he said your words are so enticing to me
i said your vibe, is that, times two
sometimes i wonder what my dreams would be like
if i slept next to you

you've managed to open me up
before you actually open me up
you've managed to enter me mentally
before you enter me physically
can your persona, style and grace
be anymore exquisitely?
it's thrilling me

but to be honest
this long distance is killing me
because i wish to no longer imagine
and for you to just be here with me

i wish to be feeling and seeing your hands really feeling me
i wish to experience your body so you can be sexually healing
me

i wish to match your rhythm
while i feel the details and inflame of your bone
i wish to take you to other dimensions
in the midst of our moans

i'm ready to satisfy your mind, body and soul
as towards me you do the same
i'm ready to give you the keys to my heart and chastity belt
to let you know i'm not playin'
but, before i continue to fantasize about us

what's your name?

if i could have you
only for a moment
if i could feel you inside of me
only for a moment
if your lips could touch my skin
only for a moment
if your sweat could intertwine with my sweat
only for a moment
if your whispers in my ear could melt my heart
only for a moment
and if being with you makes me feel something that i have never felt before
even if the feeling is
only for a moment
then i will let my intentions be known to the universe that i would want to experience all of you
for at least
one moment
because i desire to be with you
even if

it's only for a moment

his heart is my home
and i’m tired of being homesick

Kia Marlene

your love is so far away
and i'm in an unfamiliar town
where no one recognizes my soul

i'm alone

no one here can satisfy my appetite for a passionate romance
their auras are dim and their vibrations are not appeasing
only your energy can accommodate what my body desires and
what my soul requires
only your company will be pleasing
so i'm pleading

because your heart is my home and right now i feel stranded with
no road map or gps
i feel like i can't get to you
no flight
no gts

so how can i teleport to your world?
how can i reach you?
better yet
how can you reach me?

because your heart is my home and i'm ready to settle in
i'm ready to take these shoes off
my feet are exhausted from going in circles from a love that's
not even close

i'm alone

your heart is my home

and i'm tired

of being homesick

my friends say i should just move on
but how do you move on from someone that you believe is your soulmate?
how do you move on from someone that you believe may be your twin flame?

my friends say i should just get over him

but how do you get over someone
who snatched your heart without your permission?
how do you get over someone
whose energy crept up underneath your skin
and caressed every part of your existence?

my friends say i should just let him go

but how do you let him go
when you feel his spirit clinging to your heart?
how do you let him go
when you know that everything happens for a reason
these thoughts
these feels
and you know that the universe aligned this and made it all start?

so no
i'm not ready to move on
i'm not ready to get over him
and i won't be ready to let him go
until the universe sends me his replacement
(*if he's even replaceable)*

so i will allow myself to feel how i feel
until someone else enters my world and helps me to move on
i will allow myself to feel how i feel
until someone else enters my world and helps me to get over him
and i will allow myself to feel how i feel

until someone else makes it easy to let him go

until then

i won’t give up

because i truly believe

he is the one

at least for now

i want to be your favorite book
i want you to open me up and never let me go
i want you to read between my lines
highlight your favorite parts of me
inner-stand the language of my soul
look into my eyes and discover my previous editions
rub your fingertips across the words on my heart
decode the chapters of my being
study the paragraphs of my mind
allow my body to be your homework
overstand the meaning of my existence in your world
hold me as though you couldn't possibly put me down
you won't need a bookmark
because you'll never get tired of turning my pages

i want to be your favorite book

you love him, don't you?
what?
no
i don't know
i mean i guess
maybe
probably
but define love
describe love
is it the way my heart beats to the syllables of his name at the thought of his existence
or the way the butterflies created a home in the pit of my stomach because his energy still makes me nervous
or is it the way i once tried to dissolve this feeling i have for him for it to only comeback 12 times stronger

then yes
i love him
i more than love him
i'm obsessed with his essence
my heart clings to his aura
i see him in my dreams
so my subconscious he's taken over

i more than love him
i'm in love with him
i'm literally in love with him
i am inside of love with him and we are trapped here whether he knows it or not
he's the twin to my flame and we will be in love for eternity because our fire has alchemized into silk to form an untieable knot

so yes
you are right
i do love him

love him i do
him, luv?

i do

if i could mail my heart right to you i would
i would wrap it up in paper composed of poems about you
i would anoint it with my favorite fragrance just so the olfactory
receptors in your brain can get a whiff of my essence
i would seal it with a kiss containing tears of joy from you
receiving my love
i would make sure to overnight it so it'll reach you before you
woke up
i would make certain to sign it with the intentions of our souls
latching and never breaking up
if i could mail my heart right to you

i would

you've fallen in love with him
haven't you?

i'm afraid so

i want to

pick at your brain and massage your thoughts
explore the secrets that are deep down in your vault
experience your perceptions and inner-stand your beliefs
feel your soul so anxiously

swim in your emotions
to know which ones get deep
sow my feelings into your subconscious
so your love i reap

inhale your energy
and absorb your vibe
become one with you
for more than one night

whisper to your heart
so you can hear my soul
penetrate your spirit
and watch how it flow

fill my lungs with your desires
and breathe life into your dreams
stare into your eyes
to know which wounds need to be cleaned

open your mind and give you my essence
become the wind and breeze near you
for when i can't be in your presence

be the rhythm in your right brain
and the logic in your left
be the one that you need

the one your soul request

if you ever
visualize love
i hope it's me
that you see
and if your heart
plays a tune

i hope it sounds like me

i kissed him in my dream last night

not sure why he was in my dream
not sure why i experienced him in another reality
not sure why he's rooted deeply in my subconscious
or why his energy is in my thoughts

not sure why his existence makes my soul blush
or why his aura warms my heart
not sure why his bare flesh is in my imagination
or why his touch that i've never felt excites me

not sure if his being has a purpose in my world
or if mine does in his
but i kissed him in my dream last night

i wonder if our lips will lock in this one

will i kiss him in this dream?

i was in your arms last night
you held me tight
as if it were the last time you would ever hold me
i woke up
and realized it was

i haven't seen your face or felt your arms since that night
why did i have to wake up?
i would've rather stayed sleep
i would've rather chosen that dream instead of this one
because at least in that dream i'm with you

at least in that dream i'm in your arms
at least in that dream i felt loved
why did i have to wake up?
i desire to be in your arms again

you're not in this dream
so i take sleeping pills to relive it
i overdose on nyquill
just so i can search for you
feel your arms again
and feel your touch

i sleep all day and night in this dream
just so i can be awake in that dream
that dream where i don't even remember how it started
but the ending was memorable

that dream where i was in your arms
and you held me tight
as if it were the last time you would ever hold me
i guess you knew it was
i wish you would've told me

i would've fought back
and told god to let me be
i would've chosen you over life here on earth
i would've told god to let me sleep

because i desire to be in your world
more than my own

i was in your arms last night
you held me tight
as if it were the last time you would ever hold me
i woke up

and realized it was

why did you enter my life?
who gave you permission to infiltrate my thoughts?
crowd my mind?
visit my dreams?
touch my spirit?
unlock my soul?
and conquer my heart?

his vibe gave me stanzas
his existence gave me poetry

Kia Marlene

whenever i hug you
i want my soul to instantly connect to yours
and travel throughout the memories of your existence
that's stored in your being so that my mind can try to
comprehend why i'm so drawn to you

because if you were auctioning off your love
i'd be the highest bidder
i would retweet your thoughts onto my heart
as if my soul was twitter

they say opposites attract
but i feel like we're the same

are you the male version of me?
the masculine to my feminine?
yang to my yin?
spinal cord to my brain?
because i sense a connection

who are you to me?
you have left a pleasant un-dissolvable stain
on my heart from the start
what in the cosmos is happening?
why has this been arranged?

soul mate?
twin flame?

let's gaze into each other's eyes so we can figure this out

o sweet beauteous tender spirit
come close
i need you to remember me
remember the love that we experienced before now

i've been yearning so long for your presence
at one point my soul grew weary
from the search of your essence in this world
but i never gave up
i told others about how we left our splendid mark of love
throughout every lifetime that exist
but they all thought you were someone i made up

i wept during the cold nights
when your soul couldn't keep me warm
so dearest, hear me out
allow me to speak to your subconscious
where the memories of me are stored

remember me
come close

where hast thou been hiding?

i wish for you to remember my soul
and not my flesh
i wish for you to remember your time with me
remember it best

remember me

i remember you

i remember your existence throughout all of my lives

i remember when you were my husband and i was your wife

when i was your man and you were my girl
when i was your lung and you were my air
when you were the blood
and i was the vein
can't you see that despite having been many things
throughout many lifetimes
our connection and love has never changed?

so love me now in this reality
allow my energy to be a pill
that cures the amnesia you may have
from concerning what we've created
can't you see that we can't be separated

even when our lives end we will return and do this again
we will keep finding each other
no matter how many times we choose to come back to this realm
and we will fall in love again

maybe next time it will be *i* who has to remember
but can't you see that we are in this together
we made a promise eons ago to never part
so we would never hurt
that's how promises work

so remember me
because i remember you
love me again
because i love you already

let's rejoice in finding each other
since coming back here tend to always have us forget
let's celebrate love for bringing us near
because i am truly grateful that we've met

so let's fall in love once more

this is not new to us
we're good at this

look into my eyes
gaze into my soul

remember me

he asked “am i moving too fast?”
i said “no, you’re moving too slow”
i’ve been waiting for you since our last lifetime
so let’s dive all in
and allow the memories we left in the cosmic sea
from other realities
to keep us afloat

i thought of you when i was in my mother’s womb
entered this realm and forgot
but spirit made sure we met

can’t you see that the meeting of our souls was arranged
before we even chose are parents
don’t you realize the touching of our skin was arranged
before we even chose our appearance

the love we shared in previous lifetimes
overflowed in this world
and brought us here
so no, you’re not moving too fast
you’re going at the pace where we left off

don’t stop

i want to talk to you
and hear about your day
i want to listen to your heart
while on your chest i lay
i want to interlock hands
kiss your lips
and whisper into your ear
to tell you that i’ve got you, *always*
i want you to know that i won’t leave you during this lifetime
or the next

because i intend for our souls to never part ways

i want to be more than your night nurse
i want to be your daytime doctor
and your overnight healer

if the pain is getting worse
let my body be the morphine
i can be your drug dealer

regular physicals
no co-pays
let me be your health care

let me dissolve worries
erase doubts
let me show you that i care

let me massage stress out of your chest
and ease your tension with my very best
let my hands heal you and fulfill you
let my touch give you rest

let my whispers in your ears
reduce any inflammation in your being
let my whispers to your heart
induce any dopamine that you're needing

let my vibe bring you the euphoria
that you deserve to be feeling
let my aura be the prescription
that will give your body healing

let my soul and my presence
be your one and only hospital
let my existence in your world
make all things possible

let me be there for you
for the rest of your days on this earth

because i want to be

more than your night nurse

i want to give you the world
but you deserve so much more
i want to give you the universe

but that is what you already are

he said how deep can your love for me get?
i said it can get deeper than the underworld
deeper than that other girl

i would drown in the love i have for you
change forms
and resurrect as your heart

i would resurrect in your soul
i would want my essence to rise from your spine to your 3rd eye
and resurrect your energy as whole

my love would awaken the sleeping goddess within you
uncoil that serpent power
and i would watch how it flow

my love for you can get deep
where no one could ever dig it out
it would be stuck in the back of your mind
where you, yourself, wouldn't be able to get it out

my love for you can get deep
like the mathematical equation and language of the universe
that nobody has quite figured out
my love for you could change us both from the densest matter
to the lightest frequency
where, from this plane, we would have no choice
but to transfigure out

my love for you can get deep
because my desire to love you
in a million different ways is deeper
my love for you can get deep
where love itself will whisper in your ear
and tell you that i am a definite keeper
because my love gets deep

and it can get deep

for you

his love whispered into my ears
echoed throughout lifetimes
yelled my name
and found its way into my thoughts

his love gazed into my eyes
kissed my pineal
crept into my imagination
and discovered the feelings that i'd caught

his love tasted my lips
cleared passages in my chest
caressed my lungs
and became the reason i could breathe

his love penetrated my epidermis
penetrated my blood
made its way to my heart
made its way to my soul

which made its way to me

when nothing
in this world
makes sense

his existence does

sometimes
his presence
in my world

is the only thing that makes sense

her: i don't think it's healthy
for me to be thinking about you
as much as i do
it's too soon.

him: you mean, you don't think it's healthy for you
to be in love with me?
well i'm in love with you too
so if being in love with each other too soon is unhealthy

let's be sick together

i sat under a tree
with my soles in the soil
gazed at the sun
and confessed to nature
that i was in love

the winds then caused the tree
to drop its leaves
in front of me
and they spelled out your name

i guess nature already knew

nature knows it is you that i am in love with

i would like to believe
that all good things
don’t come to an end

i would like to believe
that all good things
last forever

because i want us too

you are my good thing

he said he would use all the breath in his lungs
to blow away the clouds during the day
just so it can be me and the sun
he said he would fly to the moon at night
and ask it if he can borrow the stars
just so he can give me one

he said he would rip away sidewalks with his bare hands
just so my feet can have more soil to walk on
he said he would tear down the buildings in my area
just so i can plant more trees to hug on

he said he would climb the tallest mountain
while carrying gallon sized jugs
just so he can bring me back the freshest air
he said he would build me a bird house by my bedroom window
so when i awake
birds tunes i would hear

he said he would travel far to other dimensions
just so he can bring me back the highest vibration
he said he would nickname me 'infinite'
so i can be a stranger to limitations

he said he would love me all the way into my next life
even if i forget his soul exists
he said he would place his lips on my third eye every night

so that my subconscious would remember his kiss

he was another version of me
dressed in masculinity
drenched in yang
disguised as the sun
shooting his light into me
the earth
my black hole
for me to absorb and process
as i absorbed his sacred living lux
he processed the information that his spirit felt
(that his soul felt)
distilled liquids began leaking out of his pores
i licked them to taste his alkalinity
nerve endings in my fingertips dug into his back
fingernails turned into tuning forks as i toned up his spine
in the middle of heavy rhythmic breathing i became his pilot
he was flying 1st class on board with me
ready to go on tour with me
as i was about to take him somewhere
that would be beyond the celestial

heaven

i left an impression
on your heart
with a marker that was permanent

Kia Marlene

pretty women wonder where my secret lies
why she so chill
she barely even tries
i say
it's the way i can stimulate his soul with my mind
it's the way i can penetrate the essence of his being
without opening my thighs
it's the way i can decode his existence by gazing into his eyes
it's the way i can be his strength and his peace
at the same damn time
i'm a woman
phenomenally
phenomenal woman
that's me

i walk into a room full of men and all eyes on me
not because of my beauty, it's my beautiful soul they see
it's my divine vibrations that i emit into the field they read
it's my spiritual qualities and healing energy they need
it's my ability to be a man's earth
keep him grounded
and lead him to other doors of dimensions indeed
i'm a woman
phenomenally
phenomenal woman
that's me

i walk with confidence without being conceited
i am drenched in style and grace
without extra enhancements needed
some still can't figure out my mystery
i say
i am a magnet for gods
because a goddess i be
i'm a woman
phenomenally

phenomenal woman

that's me

q. well i don't need to ask which poet inspired that poem, now do i?

a. (laughs) nope, maya angelou indeed. i love her, she inspired another one of my poems in this chapter as well.

q. so we see you can write about heartbreak and love as well as sharing your transformative journey, and we've read your poem earlier about why writers write, but besides all of that, what really inspire you to create? why do you take the time to jot down all that you experience, and all of your thoughts? why is kia marlene truly writing?

why am i writing
is what i was asked
because i have a purpose
i will stay true to my task

my soul wants to reveal something
so the pen found my hand
my thoughts need to be exposed
so i write as much as i can

why am i writing?
because this life is my journal
and i want to share with the world
i want to motivate and inspire
women
men
boys and girls

why am i writing?
because there is a story that needs to be told
and even thoughts that are not mine
will guide the pen that i hold

why am i writing?
because life is deeper than we think
my awareness is evolving
and i intend to share what i see

why am i writing?
because my curiosity led me here
i didn't think outside the box
because to me a box was nowhere

why am i writing?
at first i had no clue
but because i am divinely guided

i trust the pen that moves

why am i writing?
because spirit is using me
i am grateful for my plan
and this path for choosing me

why am i writing?
because my journey is one i intend to share
because to keep the beauty of my experiences
and transformation a secret
is just not fair

why am i writing?
because i am writing on behalf of the soul
because the weight of what's stored inside me

i can no longer hold

The Cocoon

when i feel like i have no one to talk to
pen and paper remind me that i do

Kia Marlene

so the paper stared me in the face
and the pen reached out and grabbed my hand
as i started writing they both asked
“what is it now?
what’s going on in your head?
what is it that’s on your mind?
because we can tell from the weight of your hand on this pen
and the heaviness of your wrist at the end of this notebook
that something is bothering you

so spill it

let the ink from this pen you hold run dry and run out
until you think shaking it will produce more
let the thoughts in your conscious
and the expression in your heart
allow this paper to feel it”

these lines
on which i write
which is from the tree
that was taken from nature
taken from earth
taken from me
and transformed into 2d
asked me what is going on in my dome

i replied

i don’t know
maybe it’s these lines that i see
when i look up in this dome
which roams
over the trees
over nature
over earth

over me

geo-engineered aerosols
loaded with toxic chemicals
damaging to my health
attempting to inhibit my spiritual growth
not allowing my physical and mental to transform in
and beyond 3d

or wait

maybe it's the meat
that they feed my peeps
and because my peeps don't peep
what's in their meat
it makes them weak

i'm talking mentally weak
physically weak
even the cells get weak

adjusting their structure to house pain, suffering, fear, stress,
additional artificial hormones, antibiotics and drugs
that aren't labeled on meat packages
that come frozen and preserved

the trauma is frozen and preserved
the illness is retained in its original state
so the sickness is also frozen and preserved

and then they hold hands
and give thanks
for the sickness
before it is served

now fast forward as they hold hands

and pray over a loved one
praying for healing
as they realized the sickness that tasted good to their taste buds
didn't taste good to their body
so to their body
the sickness has been served

or wait

maybe it's the religion
the religion i was born into
the religion with its different versions of books
different texts
different messages
different information
different meanings

with all of that
my curiosity grew
and penetrated the cells of my being
breaking the spell of what i was believing
bailing out my perception from the jail of limited thinking
no longer allowing my mind to be conditioned and sinking
a higher consciousness and evolved awareness
is in close reaching
as i unlearn and relearn things that the sunday school teachers
aren't teaching

i studied and explored
kemetism
gnosticism
the principles of the kabbalah
the esoteric and metaphysical interpretations of christianity
symbolism and allegoric meaning of the bible
topics that the preachers aren't preaching

as my higher self cuts the attachment
from me being born into religion
born into control
born into confusion
born into what i was taught to believe
it is done so with love

and spirituality
which is embedded in the soul that i have
starts to shine as i evolve
because it's time that i be born again
it's time that i be born from above

or wait

maybe it's the schools where we send our children
the schools that teach children what to think and not how to think
the schools that barely teach anything necessary
that will prepare one for adult life
but instead teach how to obey orders
and worship time at an early age

the schools that have a tendency to mold children
into conformists rather than encouraging children to dream
be distinctive, unique or creative from the start

the schools that preach to children about getting a job
instead of encouraging children to be entrepreneurs
and be their own boss
drilling in their minds the need for college
without mentioning the chances of actually getting a job
or the debt after graduation that will be involved

the schools that teach the children how to survive
and not how to thrive
the schools that base intelligence on IQ and SAT scores

report cards with letters and numbers on them
that's based off poorly constructed exams and tests

the schools that participate in propaganda
assisting in the undermining of society through its academics
teaching half-truths and not whole truths
teaching one sided stories
one way to learn
one way to write
one way to read
one way to do math
teaching that there is only one way

the schools that teach the same damn black history
every february, the schools that teach the same damn history in general

the past is being controlled
and because they keep teaching his story
we fail future generations
we fail to teach and/or create a new story

we fail to regenerate the past
and we fail at the chance of revitalizing the future

so maybe the weight on this pen
and the heaviness at the end of this notebook from my wrist
is heavy when i write
because these topics are not light

these topics are not to be taken lightly

they make the fast food cheap
quick service restaurants on every other street
to wheel us in and eat
then we get sick and start thinking back to what we ate last week
that made us weak
not realizing we was eating meat that wasn't meat

now we're in the doctor's office looking for a seat

i’m not against meat
i’m not against meat eaters
but i am against the harmful substances that’s
given to the animals
that ends up in the meat

Kia Marlene

q. why do you think you were a christian?

a. because my grandmother was a christian

q. why do you think your grandmother was a christian?

a. probably because her mother or grandmother was a christian

q. do you think people are attached to the religions that they are because somebody or most people in their family are also a part of that religion?

a. very much so, for most part. if my grandmother was a muslim, i'm sure i would've grown up muslim. if my grandmother or most of my family were jehovah's witnesses i'm sure i would've been that too. but at the same time, some people get attached to religion depending on their life experiences. they feel that religion, or perhaps a god outside of them, will help with their situations or life issues, so they join the church in search of something that they feel they are missing in their life, or something that they think may make their life better. they may even see a change in their life, and that's great, but for me, i parted ways with religion and grew closer to spirituality and nature. becoming spiritual oppose to religious is what made a difference in my life. that's when i saw a change within my own life, and began spending time in nature, understanding my connection to all that is. spirituality is what i was missing, spirituality is what guided me to evolve my awareness, spirituality is what led me to gain control of my life, spirituality is what led me to gain control of my own mind.

do you have control of your own mind?
or did you allow corrupt systems
corrupt governments
and mass media to own your mind and control it for you?

do you have control over your own thoughts?
or do you let the music you hear on the radio
the things you see and hear on the television and news
and the things you read in the newspapers and magazines shape
your thoughts and think for you?

have we allowed the methods of mind control
to control our very own lives?
our very own existence on this earth
controlling our feelings and actions
and how we observe and participate in this realm?

are we allowing the media's use of propaganda to influence our
beliefs, values, behaviors, emotions and attitudes?
allowing the dumbing down of our intelligence and being
uneducated about the abuse that's happening to our cerebral
cortex, the part of the brain that plays an important role in our
mental functions

are we being submissive to programming
and not being the ones who do the programming?
being harassed by and being suffers of electromagnetic
frequency mind control weapons and technologies that hijacks
the nervous system, as well as the physical body, as well as the
etheric body, and all of the subtle layers that are connected to us
while effecting brainwaves

victims of subliminal messages that's sent to the subconscious
the subconscious that stores and retrieve data
the subconscious that ensure we respond to the way it's being
programmed

the subconscious that's more powerful than our own conscious
minds

being manipulated by divide and conquer tactics
and mis-leading information
which is presented to us with the intention of influencing us
and to further an agenda

while we turn more and more into a repressive society
obeying, conforming and ignoring our power that lies inside
the power of our own being, the power that is us
the power of our own imagination
while remaining sleep and submissive to whatever

are we willingly engaging in the subtle
and non-subtle schemes of mass mind control
believing that everything we hear
and see has our best interests in mind
allowing decisions to be made for us
while believing we are independently thinking and free to decide
while our freedom of choice may actually be compromised

being led to believe
that we are choosing a solution for a problem
when the solution was created for us
way before the problem was

allowing our perception to be modified and/or distorted
being deceived on what and how to perceive
allowing our reality to be shifted and controlled
when reality is meant for us to create

bombarded with catastrophic influences
that strip our potential to think critically and logically
while not questioning the ways of the world
accepting the unacceptable

and not asking ourselves *"is mind control happening to me*
and, if so, how can i stop it, prevent it and protect myself"

it's time to become aware and recognize the damaging effects of
mind control and what it is doing
it's time to take back possession of your mind
and be the one in charge
it's time to be the architect of your own mind
and create what you wish to experience through your own lens
it's time to take back your power
it's time to take back your world
it's time to take back your life

you live in your mind

be the one who controls it

just because they want you to believe something
doesn't mean you have to

Kia Marlene

the earth is flat
duality is a trap
thoughts create
vibes attract

false flags staged
the world reacts
emotions manipulated
feelings extract

we're living in cycles
look where we at
2018?
you might want to subtract

brains are hacked
subconscious attacked
memories are zapped
more than phones are tapped

thoughts compact
power is sacked
propaganda at max
bodies and minds hijacked

balance off track

no praises to the feminine
the sun that's black

television is wack
made to distract
we're in the information age
but some minds still lack

no new age

just old info coming back

to make an impact
to get spirits intact
to reactivate wisdom
so we can know and speak facts

so codes can be cracked
so knowledge can be stacked
higher self here to assist
it's time to interact

spirit guides on the main line
it's time to contact
let's break free from mental slavery
and never look back

let's remember our power

and welcome it back

q: do you still think the earth is flat?

a: i have my theories, but at the end of the day it's up to people to do their own research and see what resonates with them. i mean, the earth may be flat, it may be the shape of a pear, it may be the shape of an egg, it may be shaped like me (laughs), it may be a dome, concave, hollow, it may be a cell that we all live inside of, it may not be an actual planet at all. all i know is that we need to take better care of her, we need to first focus on the shape that she is in, not the shape that she is. i know people who will argue you up and down about the earth being flat, but will walk past garbage on the street. let's care about the shape that earth is in and then, afterwards, expand our consciousness in caring about if there is an actual shape of earth other than what we've been told, other than what we've been showed. let's first care about the shape that she is in.

what if earth knew every time you littered
every time you spit upon her surface
every time you walked pass garbage
and didn't clean her

the grass, her hair
her skin, the pavement
we keep ourselves clean
but what are we doing for earth's maintenance?

we ignore trash on the ground like earth isn't our home
unbothered unless it's on property we own

earth can read you just like the sun
valuing myself plus honoring earth
is the perfect sum

filled with history of the universe
(just like me)
she indeed has consciousness
(just like we)

earth look out for us
but what's are outlook towards earth?

ignoring her presence
utilizing her herbs
hoping they work

without earth's trees
what fruit would we eat?
without earth's soil
what vegetable would we seek?

the lungs of the earth
indeed, are the trees

but we cut them down
then wonder why half the world has asthma
and can't breathe

but wait

still not recognizing the connection?
that you are earth
and earth has had awareness since its inception

well let me go into another direction
but first, let me ask you
when was the last time you did something for earth's well-being
and/or her protection?

if earth could talk
she'd probably ask
"what have i've done to be treated this way?
i've let you build homes
for your heads to lay

i bring forth rain
so that your crops can grow
heal your bodies when you ground
aid your connect to the cosmos

yes
i quake
produce floods
hurricanes and forest fires may start

but your home is what you make it

plus things always come back together
once they fall apart

see, i am my environment
i'm waiting on you to change
treat me how you want to be treated
for, indeed, we are the same

but when can we join together
and be on one accord?
i'm available for change
so the choice is yours

i house your lakes and oceans
so that you can sail and fish
the days where everyone cared for me
are the days that i miss

there is a need for you to express your love for me
and connect with my soul
there is a need for you to become available for my knowledge
and connect with your soles

i want you to become aware of me
because i am aware of you
as much as i want to assist in our shift
i can't do it all alone
i need you too

so no more polluting the air
no more unnatural fertilizers on my hairs
no more factories producing harmful gasses and chemicals
wrecking the ozone layer
i just want you to honor me wholeheartedly
can you do me that favor?

because i care more for you than you could possibly know
if you truly love and respect me
please let it show

for those who tend to me
my gratitude runs deep
may you care for me have a ripple effect
and wake up those who are sleep

because earth day should be everyday
and not one day in spring"

earth day should be everyday

not one day in spring

when did you surrender your thinking?
give up your expression
and lose your voice?
when did you accept control from another
give power to a person
and your right to choice?

when did you isolate yourself
separate
and disconnect from the whole?
when did you forget where you came from and who you are?
ancestral heritage stemming from the stars
when did you forget your goal?

when did you stop realizing that reality exist as a mirror
you live in your mind
this universe is holographic
and awakening to self
allows you to see things clearer

when did you stop noticing that everything you do
is a reflection of what you believe?
and that there is a much bigger picture
bigger than what you tend to experience here, in 3d?

when did you stop remembering that everything is alive
your body is your mind
and besides earth
air
fire
and water
ether
which represents the spirit and the invisible realms
made the element list go to 5

when did you stop communicating and connecting

with the cosmos and earth?
when did you stop valuing yourself
and acknowledging your worth?

when did you forget that you are indeed
one of the most greatest sources?
human beings with unlimited potential
one of the most powerful forces

when did you decide to take from earth
without participate in giving?
when did you stop expressing yourself
as multidimensional beings
and reduce yourself to linear living?

when did you stop seeing the beauty of your naturalness
and stop loving yourself just as you are?

when did you forget that you are divine
all-knowing
unlimited
and can travel far?

when did you forget that you are light disguised in flesh
and you are here for a reason?

you are more than you know

your power

it's time to believe in

still waiting on somebody to save you?
then take a number
have a seat
and grab a snickers
because only you
can save you

Kia Marlene

my mom begged me to go to church
she thinks it'll do something for me and my soul
i said it can't do nothing for me and my soul like i can

it can't save me and my soul like i can
it can't transform and evolve me and my soul like i can
it can't awaken me spiritually like i can

the true temple is the body
so why i need to go down to that temple for?
god is within
so why i need to go down to that altar for?

that altar can't do anything for me like the altar in my home can
spirit guides surrounding me
ancestors beside me
god inside me
that church can't transmute my existence like i can
like we can
that church can't transcend the ego like i can
like we can

the bible is a great book
but the preacher doesn't decode it and interpret it like i can
the choir can sing good
but the choir can't sing hymns like my restored soul can

do this in remembrance of me?
the communion at church can't help me remember
and activate christ consciousness like i can
the pastor tells folks that the doors of the church are now open
but he isn't opening them doors to other dimensions like i can
like we can

church and religion
can't assist me in realizing and utilizing my own power

like i can

my mom begged me to go to church

she thinks it'll do something for me and my soul

i went

but all it did was produce this poem

how long wilt thou sleep?
who art thou?
does thou even know?
when wilt thou arise out of thy sleep?

when wilt thou realize that this is thine life to create
and explore beyond the perceived?

oh, ye of little faith in thine own power?
do ye not believe that thou can save
and transform thine own soul
and bloom like a flower?

ye have the ability
to tap into a higher intelligence
that lies inside you
you are omnipotence, omniscient, omnipresence
but yet still in search for a god that you believe is outside of you

deliver thyself from the illusion of the physical universe
and tune in to the subjective where nothing is outside
and all is within
deliver thyself from thinking that one needs to die
to experience heaven
and that hell is a literal place
rather than a state of being
a state of mind
that one creates
but can change with new thoughts
and new intent

deliver thyself from the belief of duality
and a finite life
deliver thyself from a closed mind
and closed eyes

deliver thyself from the belief that someone outside of you will come to save you

how long

wilt thou sleep?

q. how long wilt thou sleep?

a. this is another poem written while i was in church with my mom. the pastor asked everyone to turn to proverbs chapter 6 verse 9-11, everyone stood up, and we all began reading. after i read the first five words, i zoned out and a poem came to me. once i sat back down, i began writing.

i'm not a non-believer
i just believe differently

Kia Marlene

life is really simple but we insist on making it complicated

brain washed with stress
struggle
and the need of survival
have we downgraded our intelligence since our arrival?

man-made emotions
not borne of love
not depending on self
hoping for answers from above

life is really easy
yet we create it to be hard
accepting the hand that is dealt
instead of switching the cards

fighting each other
is like fighting ourselves
crying over illusions
instead of connecting with self

won't he do it?
no, won't you do it

you have a brain waiting to be used to full capacity
won't you use it
you have data stored inside your dna and cells
you breathe in life energy
don't misuse it

you are a part of a soul
composed of memories of the whole
discover it
and don't you lose it

you are infinite intelligence
don't let society reduce it
you are the master of your world
don't let the media confuse it

life is really simple but we insist on making it complicated

buying life insurance
preparing to die
yet energy don't decease
paying for health insurance
like we're intending to get sick
but only the mind can heal
that which we term 'disease'

entertaining worry and doubt
as if they pay us
screaming life isn't fair
as if life betrayed us

complaining about illusionary problems
as if problems said *"rate us"*
talking about it's genetics
as if genetics really make us

life is really simple but we insist on making it complicated

stop
look
and listen

be still
stay chill
and discover your mission

use your facial muscles to smile instead of frown

meditate
diffuse some oils
and clear out any blocked energy of the chakras
from root to crown

let your intuition guide for you
let earth provide for you
tune in
connect
and let your higher self ride for you

look into the mirror
directly into your eyes
and say “i do all things with ease”
say “i can do all things through christ consciousness
which strengthens me”

life is really simple but we insist on making it complicated

start to live up to who you truly are
this is your life
it’s time to know your power

it’s time to activate it

sitting here with the desire to explore my bloodline
intending to inner-stand the power of the individual
global
and galactic mind

double dutching
through timelines
leaving prints
no crime

wanting to enhance
decode
and unfold the strands of my dna

water the seeds of my thoughts
certify
nurse
and assist them
no cna

appreciating all the nanoseconds of my existence
embracing all change with no resistance

feeling grateful to be back on earth
alive
and fully aware
in this divine human temple that i chose

feeling grateful to be back on earth
alive
and fully aware

to watch my awareness unfold

i came from nothing to something?
no, i came from something to greater
matter of fact
greater to greatest
every day i sun gaze
so i'm receiving the latest

i didn't start from the bottom
i started at the top
society might've brought who i am a little down
but i brought it back up

and since my consciousness changed
let me tell you what i've gained

i've gained a sense of who i am
and the reason that i'm here
i've gained unison with all that there is
and for all consciousness i started to care

i've gained self-empowerment
and obtained more enlightenment
i've gained a love for life
and, for each new day
a new excitement

i've gained clarity about my existence
and a realization of my self-worth
i've gained a deep love for my being
and a deeper love for earth

i've gained a peace of mind
and vision to notice the signs
i've gained a connection with all things
all things divine

i've gained wisdom from ancient papers
and an enjoyment with nature
i've gained a realization that i am a part of something grand
a part of something major

i've gained high vibrational thoughts
and high vibrational behaviors
i've gained closeness to self
and that has been a game changer

awareness evolved
perception changed
transformation occurred

Kia Marlene

don't be afraid to change
change is inevitable
change is necessary

let's elevate
gravitate
become spiritual seekers
participate in a spiritual evolution
remembering our wholeness
no fragmentary

time to become inflicted with a new stimulus
a desire to inner-stand our being
its connections and its purpose
rearrange our thoughts and environment
to rearrange our genetic make up
recreate new subjects in the mind
giving the subconscious a whole new syllabus

let's step outside the boxes we grew comfortable in
reevaluate and revise the infinite spheres of our mind
revamp our intelligence and creativity
while adding gems to the field

let's take a chance and advance
be willing to allow for brain wave frequencies to drop to a trance
so we can enter the gateway of higher consciousness
imagine a land flowing with coconut milk and raw honey
while being in control of the crops it yields

let's stop thinking in 3d and start feeling in the 5th
and start using the chakra of the 5th
to self-express and converse with the element known as the 5th
about how we desire an awakened nation

let's be observant of our mind's garden

plant high vibes if none seeded
and if present
low vibrational plants
must and will be weeded

let's fly above mediocre
and become the architects of our minds
let's design greatness
and realize that life will be easy
once we put all fear behind

let's return to nature
let's return to the source

let's assist the shift in consciousness of the world
while embracing our never-ending course
using the greatest feeling of them all

love, the greatest force

one soul
many spirits

one message
will many hear it?

Kia Marlene

i agreed to come back here
knowing that i would consciously forget everything

that's bravery
that's courage

i must've been really passionate about the mission

and while i'm here
remembering all that i once knew

as everything slowly comes back to me

i won't ever stop

being passionate about the mission

they say the future is plastic
so i will bend it in my favor
about to get off at the 13th floor
shout-out to the evolution elevator

to the people that's vibing low
i guess i'll see you later
or, maybe i won't
because your frequency is less than greater

i'm at the bar of enlightenment
drinking shots of growth with no chaser
grew to realize money don't like to be chased
so no, i don't chase her

rev. ike taught me that money is here to serve me
realized how grand i am
and said abundance deserve me

new beliefs got seeded
patiently waited to see how they'd bloom
stood firm
didn't fold
because i knew the universe would come through

trusting my journey
with my guides by my side
enjoying each moment
being my own ride or die

because first i will ride
learn and grow
then i will die
transform from the old

on the way to the top

your company must be like minded individuals
can't hang with those that sleep
if your eyes have been opened to a different kind of visual

on my way further up
and those i leave behind
to come with me
i won't change my mind

best thing i can do to help them out
is to continue to evolve

and focus on mine

people said i changed
i did more than change
i transformed

Kia Marlene

somebody asked me, “what’s new?”
i replied, “a new perception of life
new knowledge
new light”

somebody asked me, “where have you been?”
i replied, “hibernating
distant from the outer world
and active with the inner me”

somebody asked me, “what happened?”
i replied, “change
transformation
new information obtained
new insight gained
same journey, different lane”

somebody asked me, “what happened to your motivation?”
i replied, “it never left
i just switched it
can’t stay the same if my consciousness shifted
my awareness has expanded
so my thoughts, ideas and purpose have altered and lifted”

somebody asked me, “what’s your inspiration?”
i replied, “earth
myself
my younger and higher self
all of humanity
the power that be
invisible forces that do all they can for me”

somebody asked me, “what’s your intention?”
i replied, “to be light
always be available to receive light
and to continue to share light with all that i encounter”

when was the last time you followed your spirit
and talked to your soul?
when was the last time you trusted your intuition
and recognized what it could hold?

can you remember who you were
before your brain got washed?
can you remember your mission
before another was taught?

distractions are meant to keep you off track
not seeking answers within
are meant to keep you on lack

lack of knowledge
lack of knowing
lack of self
the essence of your being knows it all
seek no more
from anyone else

listen to and understand your emotions
when you start feel them
be aware of life lessons
when self reveals them

don't get too caught up
in the illusions that you're seeing
they're just projections in your world
with a much grander meaning

use your eyes
to see what the picture tries to hide
use your ears
to hear the voice that resides inside

rediscover your path
and don't follow the paths of others
rediscover that you are here to explore
experience
mature
and to love one another

remember who you are
remember your goal

follow your spirit

talk to your soul

nature and all of earths inhabitants has ears
from the trees
to the sun
the water
and insects
they all can hear

i have many conversations with nature
and all that there is
but it wasn't until i saw a beetle crawling
i started to speak to it
it stopped to listen
and that brought tears

it was in that moment
i further realized
we are all the same thing
in different forms

we are all energy
calling earth our home

made of the same substance

with different norms

i was alone

but for the first time
it didn't feel like it

nature was my company

i conversed with the trees
danced with the wind
had staring contests with the sun
the ocean played me a song
the birds sang the chorus
i exchanged thoughts with the moon
told jokes to the stars
spirits from the ether whispered in my ear
"*you are never alone*"

and for the first time

it didn't feel like it

what do we lose by talking to plants?
nothing.
yet we gain so much when we do

Kia Marlene

what if my plants are my ancestors?
what if they passed on
changed forms
and came back
this way?

what if spirit led me to crack open that pit
grab that mango seed
germinate it
and turn it back into life
this way?

did i just assist a mango with reincarnation?
were my ancestors waiting to be born again
to return to this dimension
this way?

did my ancestors sense my progress
know that soon i'd be able to understand their language
and feel their vibrations from plant life
this way?

did some of my ancestors choose to comeback as plants
so that they could produce sound waves to raise my frequency
bring ancient wisdom to communicate to me
which would further assist in my growth and transformation
this way?

i know plants have feelings
so i express my love towards them every single day
so if my plants are my ancestors
i'm grateful for the form they chose

even if

it's this way

the thicker the hair
the deeper the roots

Kia Marlene

people see the wild hair and say
oh, she has let herself go
but i see it as i've let myself be
i've escaped from the prison of caring what others think
i've set myself free

free from the beauty standards of this world
free from the ideas of society
decided to be more like myself
because being and looking like others no longer excited me

decided to devote less energy to the styling of my hair
don't really care who stares
because me and my hair
part nervous system
part antenna
are busy using our energy to send
and receive signals through the air

people see the wild hair and say
oh, she has let herself go
yes, i've let myself go
to another level of inner-standing
another level of awareness
a level of unidentifiable identity
a new level of rareness

my purpose and who i am is becoming more visible
so sorry
not sorry
if the grooming of my hair is becoming less visible

the thicker the hair
the deeper the roots
allowing my hair to be unique and express itself on its own
while parts of my heritage shine through

so if my hair looks wild
it's because the extension of my nervous system
is unmanipulated and untamed
to be great and divine

magical
intelligent
creative
special
vital and wild

is exactly

how my hair can be defined

what am i supposed to smell like?
a bunch of artificial ingredients
labeled on the back of smell good products
that i can't pronounce?

i prefer my scent
my friends in the cosmos say i don't smell like most humans
so they come around often
and their presence they announce

my unique aroma
allows me to come into contact
with all things of divineness

my scent
my essence
i embrace all of me
i will not hide this

i will not allow my magnetism to be attacked and suppressed
by slathering harmful chemicals onto my skin
that rapidly enters my bloodstream
for the sake of what's popular
and what's appealing to society

i will only allow my natural scent to flourish and communicate
as it travels and influence
and subconsciously sends out and attract high vibrations
as i am now aware of how my body's own natural perfume
gives me power
which it is abundantly supplying me

so if reality is powered by scent
then mine will be notable
so i can be available for divine arrangements
and if my aura encases smell

then mine will produce and radiate energy
that's exclusive and fragrant

but still, i ask

what am i supposed to smell like?

a bunch of artificial ingredients
labeled on the back of smell good products
that i can't pronounce?

peanut butter jelly sandwich and ice cream
never thought it would make my heart smile
and my soul scream

my soul screamed *yes, finally*
we haven't tasted this since we were about 5 or 13
the soul loves ice cream
but with all the information i was ingestion
the conscious mind determined it was bad for me
and bread was a no-no
because i got hooked on certain diets
and went gluten free

but, isn't everything an illusion anyway?
isn't nothing either good or bad
but thinking makes it so
anyway?

not once have i had thoughts that said
"what am i doing? i shouldn't be eating this"
i've only had thoughts of love, joy and happiness

if my thoughts were
"this is bad, i'm going to pay for this"
then the body would've responded accordingly
but i was grateful for the moment
commanded my body to execute divine harmonious digestion
because that's how tight the bond between my mind and body be

i know almond milk ice cream is good
and i've had gluten free bread before
but mr. softee ain't selling dairy free ice cream on his truck
and gluten free bread is not being sold at the corner store

so if i craved it
the soul desired it

no regrets
in fact, i admired it

i admired the fact that i could eat something
that i normally wouldn't
and not feel bad
i think my new beliefs about the mind and diet won this round
while old beliefs finished last

not saying i will eat peanut butter jelly sandwiches
and ice cream everyday
but when i desire it
and the soul crave it
i will fulfill without guilt
without caring about what anybody say

but isn't everything an illusion anyway?

if i owned a school
i would plant a huge garden next to it
and the children would learn how to grow fruits and vegetables
and the cooks would use fresh produce to prepare the children's meals

if i owned a school
everything in the cafeteria would be non-gmo
non processed
organic and local
we would have fresh pressed juice
and the water would be a choice of fresh spring
alkaline or distilled

if i owned a school
the children would sit with their legs crossed during breakfast
and lunch for better digestion
they would be seated on bean bags in the classroom
and there would be no ela testing

if i owned a school
the children would practice walking backwards
for mental benefits and better blood circulation
i would have the children work on sudoku puzzles
and play brain games
for better hemisphere integration

if i owned a school
i would have the children learning about the law of attraction at an early age
they would be tested on different universal laws
learn how to write business plans and be entrepreneurs
and they would be taught to always choose happiness
over staying at a stressful job just because of its high wage

if i owned a school

all the children would learn and practice yoga
jujitsu
and qiqong
i would have comedians visit weekly
and we would find ways to laugh throughout each class
and start each day with pharell's happy song

if i owned a school
it would be filled with fresh flowers
and air cleaning plants
children would sun gaze every morning
and they would never be allowed to say the word can't

if i owned a school
children will be barefoot on the grass during recess to soak up
earth's beneficial negative ions
and give new meaning to the word grounded
hugging trees would be mandatory
studying sacred geometry and chakras is a must
and they would enjoy the solfeggio frequencies while learning
what each sound is

if i owned a school
we would listen to fela kuti
bob marley
soca music
beethoven
and mozart

the children would learn how to write poetry
and be able to express their thoughts and feelings
through any kind of art

if i owned a school
i would teach the children how to write with their non-dominant
hand

and in cursive too
we would say positive affirmations daily
learn how to play chess
and learn more than one foreign language *(at least two)*

if i owned a school
the children would never hear the word ‘failing’
they would learn that the mind and body are one
and while being taught a great deal of knowledge

they would still have fun

detoxing from people
is also good for your health

Kia Marlene

i need to detox from you

i no longer want to ingest your words
see your avatar
or feel your soul

i no longer want to hear your deep vocal tone
smell your scent
or be close enough to taste your thoughts

i no longer want to digest and absorb your electromagnetic field
visualize your imaginations
or touch your dreams

it's time i detoxify you from my subconscious mind
dry brush your skin cells from my flesh
cleanse my dna of the emotions i developed
because of your energy
it's time i start fresh

i need

to detox

from you

q. oh, so we're detoxing from people now?

a. yup (laughs). detoxing from anything and anyone that doesn't come from a place of love, involve love, or allow me to feel loved. i can't confine love to one chapter because love is a part of the journey, love is all that there is; love is forever flowing, flowing through my heart, through my mind and through the field which is accessible for me. and the best love that exist is the love from one's self. throughout this entire journey i have been reminded that the greatest love of all is the love that i discovered within me, the love that i give myself, and the type of love where i can go look into the mirror and realize it is love that i see, love that is me.

but.... sometimes i get into my feelings and have to be reminded of that (laughs).

atlantic starr tells us
we'd better answer when love call
but i'm starting to think love doesn't have my
number in its contact list

Kia Marlene

sometimes i feel like i've been stood up by love
i remember the first time that my heart broke
love said "this won't be the last of me
i'll be back, just take some time to heal"
years went by
i called up love and said "hey love, i'm healed
i'm ready for you"
that was on love's voicemail
love never called back
months went by
i called again and said "love i feel like you're avoiding me
there's no one here with me
where are you hiding?
you said you'd come back for me"
in the middle of me leaving another voicemail
love picked up, finally, and said "i am back"
i replied "no you're not because i'm still single
i'm still alone"
love replied "you're not alone
i'm here and been brought you somebody"
i replied "seriously?"
"where?"
love replied

go look in the mirror

i thought love had abandon me
til i looked in loves eye and saw my reflection

wow, i said
love look a lot like me
love is eternal like me
love is ongoing like me
transcending time and space like me

love, sweet love
sweeter than the most purest unfiltered honey
the love i have for you
matches the love that sunflowers have for the sun
on the days when it is sunny

i feel love every time my belly expands
cave in and breath leaves my nostrils
i feel love every time my hand is placed on my heart
and its precious sound becomes my favorite gospel

so no
love has not abandon me
i feel love when my heart beats
i feel love when i breathe
i feel love when i draw close to a mirror and gaze into my eye
and see that it's love that i am

love, which is me

he asked me
if i was seeing anybody
i replied *yes*
i'm seeing myself

i'm seeing myself in love with who i am
obsessed with who i'm becoming
happy and at peace
all while self-awareness increase

so yes
i'm seeing someone
i'm seeing myself

for the first time

i'm finally seeing me

when i go on a date
i don't want to discuss who was shot by the cops
or the latest in the news
i'd rather discuss sun gazing
and what, if any, rituals you do for the full moon

let's talk about metaphysics
if ufos are real
and if we think the earth is flat
let's discuss sidereal astrology
the longest fast we ever did
and where are the stores with the seeded watermelons at

when i go on a date
we don't always have to go out to eat
or to the movies
let's take long hikes
walks by the water
picnics in nature
allowing the vibrations around us to be penetrating and soothing

let's talk about psychedelics
and how strong we think are intuition is
let's discuss occult science
and what we think our true purpose is

when i go on a date
i want to discuss the books or documentaries
that caused change in our lives
let's discuss the importance of a balanced diet
and what keeps us up at night

let's talk about our favorite movies
our favorite comedians
and who's our favorite storytelling rapper
let's discuss our favorite quotes

favorite authors
and any life lessons that we think we've mastered

when i go on a date
i want to talk about lucid dreaming or out of body experiences
and if we ever decoded the dreams we have at night
let's share at least one thing that others don't know about us
and compare our favorite affirmations we recite

let's not talk about future goals
and where we see ourselves 5 years from now
let's embrace the moment
live in the present
because the only thing that matter
is right here
and right now

q. so this might be off topic, but since you mentioned story telling rappers, i must ask: when did you fall in love with hip hop?

a. (laughs) to be honest, even though this song was way before my time and i was already loving and listening to hip hop in general, i fell in love with hip hop when i heard funky 4+1 "that's the joint." that will forever be my jam, that song made me wish i was around during that era of hip hop. like i said before, i was already loving the hip hop during my time while growing up, but when i heard that song for the first time i was like "oh, okay, they going in" (laughs). definitely one of my all-time faves and it really puts me in a good mood when i hear it.

q. oh, ok, so you're old school i see. does that mean you like older men?

a. (laughs). being old school does not mean i only like older men. i like who i like, i don't discriminate, i don't even have a type…

or wait…

maybe i do.

he asked me what my type was
he said “you look as though you like them tall and dark”
i replied “i like them conscious and intelligent
their height and complexion to me is irrelevant
does he know thyself?
love himself?
any signs of spiritual development?

how does he treat his mother?
better yet, how does he treat mother earth?
does he know his value?
his connection to the whole?
does he know his worth?

i don’t care about whether his clothes are name brand
but does he know how to repair, activate
and evolve all 12 dna strands?
if he wanted to right now
could he go and buy land?
and how decalcified is his pineal gland?”

he said “you look as though you like them street smart”
i replied “street smart is cool, but is his mind smart?
does he know the 42 ideals of ma’at
the 12 universal laws
the laws of nature
can he deprogram and reprogram his subconscious
and rewire his brain?
does he know his birth chart?

is he aware that he is infinite consciousness in human form?
and that those chemtrails in the sky are not the norm?

i couldn’t care less about the rap songs that he can muffle
but i do care if he at least heard of
neville goddard

rev. ike
manly p. hall
napoleon hill
alan watts
krishnamurti
dr. sebi
oscar wilde
terence mckenna
ernest holmes
or walter russell

my type is the type with his chakras balanced
full of wisdom
aware
happy
and achieving goals

the type that's consciously living
spiritually ascending
and respecting his temple
by not filling it up with gmo's

so i'm not basing my type off his looks and physicality
i'm basing it off his vibes
his way of thinking
his inner self
his intellect
his charm
the way he percieves
and his unique strong personality"

my library is bigger than my shoe collection

Kia Marlene

i made love to information
the orgasm sent me to another dimension
i came back and realized i was light

9 months later
i gave birth to a new consciousness
no c-section
veil got lifted
now i don't see sections

separation is an illusion
there is no separation of cells

nurtured my new awareness
with ancient wisdom
symbols
love
limitless thoughts
and everything that felt real

watched my awareness grow and evolve
like a caterpillar to a butterfly
flying off in this cosmic sea of reality

flying off to higher planes of existence

flying off

so earth
and all of humanity

can witness

knowledge is the key
but applied knowledge is using that key to open doors

Kia Marlene

q. so, would you say a lot of transformation took place during this stage?

a. indeed. a lot of transformation and hibernation took place during this stage, a lot of separation from the outside world, a lot of focusing on myself and further figuring out my reason for being here. i truly believe that without my hibernation and separation not much transformation would have occurred, so i am grateful for how everything played out. i am grateful for all of the information i accumulated and everything that resonated with me.

q. why did you decide to name this chapter "the cocoon"?

a. well, besides the fact that that's the stage that follows the caterpillar stage (laughs), when the caterpillar stops eating, it then hangs upside down. in my case, though, i didn't hang upside down, i was hanging by myself. the caterpillar then spins itself a cocoon, a protective casing--my isolation was my protective casing, my protection from the possibility of not evolving. within the cocoon the caterpillar radically transforms its body--i transformed, i transformed my mind and my body, and because of that transformation, because of that stage, because of my isolation and a search for all that is stored within me and all that i embody, something beautiful happened.

q. and what was the beautiful thing that happened?

a. a butterfly was able to emerge.

thoughts that i never wrote
stanzas that i never spoke

from the paper
to the words
from my brain
down to my soul

were these words buried deep within
and resurrected through the decalcifying pineal gland
once i searched within
thoughts rose
once my mind rose
visions and expressions rose to the surface and utilized the pen

the pen that would convey my strongest feelings
from my mental
onto 2d surface
intending to aid anyone in an awakening
while composing rhymes about my soul's progress as my service

i hope it's worth it

i'm sure it is

because spirit told me that i'm needed

i had to unplug
detach
grow
evolve
seek and mature
so i could remember that the plant of super-consciousness
within me was already seeded

i watered it with solitude and questions for my cells

weeded out limits
became mindful of auto-suggestions
improving communication with myself

i became available for all this information from the cosmos
that was being thrown at me
intended for my body to receive it
convert and house it
and allow it to inflame through my being like acne

all so i can send it back out through my thoughts
and the stanzas that i never spoke
and share my light with the world
so i could assist in shifting a new level of reality
and observe as humanity's awareness unfurled

The Butterfly

it feels so good to look in the mirror and say
"damn, i really love myself"

Kia Marlene

i looked in the mirror and said

your love is queen
your love is infinite
your love is divine
your love is everything

your love is the highest of the high
the brightest of the bright
your love makes my heart sing

your love is whole
your love is truth
your love penetrates my cells
and keeps me grounded
the deepest root

your love is divine energy
caressing all parts of the inner me
your love plus my growth
produces the greatest chemistry

your love has transformed me
your love has informed me
your love melted away thoughts that produced a cold heart
your love has warmed me

your love is real
your love can heal
your love is beyond what i imagined
giving my soul that whip appeal

your love is peace
your love is joy
your love is magnificent
and all that i'll ever need

your love is peace
your love is joy
your love is magnificent
and all that i'll ever need

real love
self-love

love

from me

when you love yourself
it shows
everyone will start to know
loving yourself is good for yourself
it's good for your soul

your cells will start to notice
your subconscious will take notes
your whole environment will change
and inner peace will start to grow

every part of your being will scream thank you
you'll create room to thrive

loving yourself is the greatest feeling ever

and you'll truly feel alive

once i fell in love with myself
i fell in love with the whole universe

Kia Marlene

it's me vs. me
i'm the only player in this tournament
i refuse to go back to old ways
intending for my growth to be permanent

the universe taking orders for a higher consciousness
i asked for a whole case
higher self showing me the map of enlightenment
i asked can i trace

spirit stirring up awareness
i asked can i taste
earth growing flowers of information
i asked can my mind be the vase

the cosmos handing out transformation
so i reached out to the firmament

and what don't involve growth

i'm really not concerned with it

advertisements on phones
tell us to tap here
to download apps
but when will we tap within
to receive downloads
from places that's not seen on maps?

i know i am not alone
for there are spirits living in my walls
plants that talk to me
beings from other dimensions knocking at my door
ancestors running through my veins
spirit guides jointed at my hip
spirit animals roaming through my field
whispers from the moon in my ears during the night
forehead kisses from the sun
that reaches my pineal during the day
the wind gives me hugs
the birds give me songs
nature gives me flowers
the smoke from my palo santo gives me messages
higher self gives me wisdom
younger self offers advice
angelic beings send support

so no

i am not alone

this is my peace

gazing at the sun
as it shines on me
trees waving with their branches
and their leaves
the sound and touch
of strong winds and gentle breeze
birds flying by
singing songs to me
my feet touching wet mud
and dew from morning's grass
conversing with nature
enjoying mother earth
i want this moment
to forever last

people think it’s weird that i like to lay in the sun
and stare at it
i think it’s weird that they don’t

Kia Marlene

sometimes i get mad at the clouds for blocking the sun
i tell them “move back
you can’t keep him for yourself
you’re not even real”
the clouds ignore me and don’t tolerate my anger

so i close my eyes
imagine the sun on me once more
i soon feel heat on my skin
and sweat leaving my pores

because imagination is a weapon

that even the clouds can’t compete with

she was kissed
but it wasn't an ordinary kiss

as she was kissed she felt heat surge throughout her being
she felt blood spin and dance throughout her veins
she heard her organs play a harmonic tune
her eyes closed and she saw a rainbow of 13 colors
and a field of sunflowers

she smelled the aroma of fresh air
and felt it massage her lungs
she heard the tune of love
as the universe began to sing its melody
she opened her eyes
and was able to describe the clear color of light

a gentle breeze maneuvered through each individual eyelash

this kiss came from who?
this kiss came from where?
not from the old man's son
but from the one main sun

with each peck
her cells became more intelligent
with each peck
her purpose became clear and more relevant

thoughts were exchanged
a higher shift in consciousness was arranged

no gazing
eyes closed
still allowing it to kiss her third eye

no clothes on

body bare

allowing it to kiss her whole mind

some say you're an illusion
but i still feel your heat
i don't intend to worship you
but be grateful for the energy you bring

you're more than a burning form of gas
your rays charge the cells
and allow my skin to make vitamin d

you do more than light up the day
you strengthen immune systems
while providing healing with ease

i'm thankful for my thick skin
its ability to absorb your rays
and store them as information and energy
i'm thankful that i can receive your light and store it
as you charge me inwardly

you're an information center
living light
you permit and activate life
to not fear you
but embrace you
is only right

no sunglasses on
wouldn't want to starve the brain
i'm trying to stimulate the pineal
and experience greater vision obtained

i intend to keep my conscious clear
so i can house your divine energy
as you penetrate the layers of my epidermis throughout the day

i intend to always expose myself to you

so i can improve my health
and my ability to evolve strands of my dna

seeing you shine through them clouds
and being in the presence of your light
i feel reassured that everything will be okay

i feel the strength that you send
the guidance you provide
the nourishment you bring
and the comfort from your rays

if i ever feel alone
i go outside
i look up
and know that i'm not

i let your essence hit my spine
stimulate my mind
and illuminate all that i got

i mean all that i embody
all that i am

not sure if you are hollow
powered by cold fusion
or have advance civilizations living inside you
but i'm grateful for your energy

even if you are a hologram

what if doctors prescribed sunshine
time in nature
and laughter?

what if more doctors cared about their patients
rather than big pharma
and the money that it's after?

true healing is mental
psychological
emotional
and spiritual
way beyond the physical

yet some of us eat all the alkaline food in the world
but still lack self-love
kindness
and inner peace
while showing signs of feeling miserable

we can't heal scars of the flesh
without also healing scars deep within the mind
not realizing that oftentimes it is we who create dis-ease
with worrying, fear, anger
and even unhealthy environmental factors
which can affect us for a longtime

the holistic approach is cool
but we still have to be mindful of our thoughts and attitudes

we going gluten free
but are we going worry free?
avoiding dairy
but do we avoid negativity?

what we eat is only a fraction of what we ingest

we ingest what we see
what we read
and what we listen too
so tell me, how well do you digest?

because there aren't any enzymes being sold in stores
to help digest the low vibrations
we choose to ingest and absorb

we need to isolate
forgive
love
seek within
make peace
and get back to nature
if we truly want to heal and transform

it's time to nourish and take care of our cells
it's time to heal on a cellular level
it's time to detox the body and the mind
it's time to cherish and honor our divine vessel

so no more disrespecting the temple (*physically and mentally)*
no more forgetting that we can be our own healers
who can heal the physical and mental
throughout any lifetime

let's practice true self-care

let's stop neglecting and abusing

the body and the mind

they teach you how to live
and may even teach you how to die
but do they teach you how to fly?
do they teach you how to ascend?
do they tell you that you can take your body with you
to the very very end?
ok, scratch that
my bad
there is no end

but do they teach you that you can rise by going within?
this might be hard to grasp
but you have the power to make your body last
you don't have to go 6ft under
or turn your body into ash

you can take your body along
awaken to pure consciousness
function in higher dimensions
and mesh with the one soul
you have options
there are other realms you can go

ask yourself
how can i unlock my brain for full use?
how can i prepare my cells
and my body to raise its vibrational frequency
switch it from the densest matter to the lightest
so i can take my embodiment when i'm done here to any
dimension that i choose?

teach me
show me
i intend to experience this

to be able to leave

and, if i want, come back to this 3d plane
continue to interact with beings on earth
with an accelerated awareness
without reincarnation
without a new ego
without relearning what i already know
and without reliving the programming of social consciousness

but if i choose not to come back here
i'll be grateful for the experience

the ability to make a conscious decision
to engage further in evolution
to shift my cells
experience activated dna
raise my energetic frequency
and to consciously gravitate towards greater
which is the task

teach me how to take my physical body into the higher realms
to make the complete dimensional shift into another reality

teach me how to ascend

teach me how to consciously

return to the vast

rest in peace?
no, nothing rests
we don't even rest when we sleep
so how about we say transition in peace
or transform in peace

because when i transition out
don't tell me to rest in peace
i am not resting

i've just transformed
experiencing another realm
returning in another form
or doing more questing

death is not to be feared
but is something to try understand, right?
because when we understand death
we understand life
and when we understand life
we understand that nobody dies, right?

what if everybody on earth realized that death is not real
and we are immortal?
that's a shift right there
what if everybody on earth realized that they don't lose life
they just gain consciousness?
plot twist right there

what is created can never be destroyed
acknowledging that you are deathless
is something that you truly can't avoid

death is something they've sold to us
and people buy it up like life insurance

death is something they've sold to us
and people buy it up like life insurance

so can we change our perception please?
there is only life after life once we leave
let's get rid of the illusion
and end the confusion

your life is ongoing

your story has no conclusion

living by 42 laws
so that my heart is lighter than a feather
when they weigh it on the scale

no way i'm coming back
although mother earth
has treated me very well

i'm ready to evolve

i have other duties to fulfill

i am a vessel
copper colored to be exact

loaded with melanin
scent like cinnamon
drenched in intelligence

superconductor of electricity
9 ether hair

got connections with beings that are close
and beings that aren't even here

meaning they're in a different galaxy
they're in a different reality
meaning i'm no longer only occupying 10% of my brain's
capacity

down here spiritualizing matter
while avoiding unnecessary chatter
enjoying the fact that both my power and my consciousness
evolved and climbed their ladders

no longer a slave to my thoughts
i am the master of my mind
i preached to the serpent at my base to awaken it
i am the pastor of my spine

as it rose
i rose
awareness enhanced
and i remembered that i descended to ascend

and when i say stay woke
i'm talking to myself
the creative fire that rose through me

the born power that resides within

being human is cool
but becoming superhuman is the goal

Kia Marlene

what if you were a potato
and someone peeled you with the sharpest blade
chopped you up with the sharpest knife
threw you into ice cold water
tossed you into hot sizzling grease

then from the grease to the paper towel
then from the paper towel to the plate

a plate in front of a hungry being who has not yet ate
a hungry being who is ready to devour you
and make your existence vanish
without appreciation for your energy

and without a mere thanks

what if?

q. let me guess, you were making french fries?

a. (laughs) yup. i had thought to myself, how many of us actually give thanks to the food? we grew up with the ‘god is good, god is great’ grace, buy how many of us thank the actual food for its energy? how many of us thank the food for allowing us to experience it? how many of us thank the food for all that it has been through in order to make its way to us? picture everyone giving thanks to their food, wouldn’t that be beautiful? it’s ok to change the way we say grace, or add to it, giving thanks to the food is giving thanks to the source, it’s all energy.

you don't have to be a model to take model pictures
because when you think about it
we are all already models
models of all that there is

models of love
models of immortality
models of a perfect design

models of the universe
models of beauty
models that's divine

so if you don't think you are the universe
i'm here to tell you that you are the moon, sun and stars
and if you don't think that you are beautiful

i'm here to tell you that you are

happiness is a drug that everyone should be hooked on

Kia Marlene

if those that live off the frequencies i produce
don't like the sweet taste of love
then they won't survive

if they are not keen on ingesting joy
then they won't stay alive
and if they don't crave peace
happiness
and bliss
then they cannot feed off of i

i am a frequency generator
only generating vibes that are high
generating vibes that can't be lowered
even if other energies tried

these vibes are alive
these vibes cannot die
these vibes are wave patterns
not straight
no lye

no johnny gill
but these frequencies i transmit got the ether singing
"my, my, my"
no nsync
but these energies that have an appetite for fear
can't eat what i serve
so i've got them singing
"bye, bye, bye"

if vibrational frequencies were considered fashionable
then mine would, indeed, be fly
if low vibrational frequencies are considered immature
then i'm only producing vibes that are ripe

if my energy is being harvested
then those who intend to reap
will only find crops of love, joy and bliss

because high vibrations within me

is something that will always exist

i can tell that my presence
triggered something in your subconscious
because you looked at me
as if my mind held your thoughts hostage
you looked at me as if i affected your nerves
and caused in you an electrical blockage
you looked at me as if i'd sent a threat to your ego
and you were unable to block it
what sparked those eyes and the jittering of your hands?
what sparked the tense energy and sweat from your glands?
why does my vibration cause you to tremble?
it's almost as if the cat's got your tongue down in limbo
no need for you to speak because i've felt all you have to say

but why does my presence make you feel this way?

there's life in you
as i light my incense
your energy i witness
your bright orange yellow color
starting with blue
i feel your heat
thought is heat
you are consciousness
you are light
when i speak
you hear me
when i look at you
you see me
it feels good to be conscious
of the consciousness of your flame
your smoke can travel through dimensions
so i send messages to you
as you dance throughout the ether
the burning of matter
allow things to change forms
you take life and give it
a powerful force
that can destruct
and create
your bright flames have awareness
to understand you is to be fearless
i've watched you transform people and substance
i've watched you manifest things as well
from fire
smoke
to producing ashes
the trinity of your being exist in continuation
i gaze at your blaze
mesmerized by your rage
a flame defined as a hot glowing body of ignited gas
that is generated by something on fire

sounds a lot like me
my ancestors sang and danced around you
as they held ceremonies in your name
people trust you with their camp stories
and their list of things they want to let go of
without you how could i clear energies with the smoke from my sage?
without you how could anyone blow out birthday candles and celebrate a new age?
you give life to anything that needs to be lit
powerful
magical
and necessary to exist

we are consciousness.
up to 60% or more of our body is water
so what makes you think that the water you are
aware of
is not also aware of you?

Kia Marlene

what if you were trapped in a dark pipe
unable to see any light
until a being twisted a knob
allowing you to see life

only for life to ignore you
not give you attention or a simple hello
not show you love
not show you compassion
or be grateful for your flow

what if you felt used and unappreciated
with no one ever telling you "thanks for keeping me clean
thanks for allowing me to wash away the day
thanks for the serenity
thanks for the peace"

what if the water from your shower just wanted to feel love
and not just your skin
what if i told you that you have the power to remove any
possible fluoride and chlorine that it may carry within

your thoughts and vibrations
can affect the molecular structure of water
because water has consciousness just like you

so next time you're in the shower
speak life to it
send it some love

send it some gratitude

q. so let me guess, you were in the shower when you thought of this poem?

a. yup (laughs). but all jokes aside, i really love all water. water has consciousness, it's alive just like us, and whenever i think of it i always extend my love and gratitude to the water that i drink, that i bathe in, cook with, water my plants with, etc. but to be honest, before i wrote this poem i never paid much attention to my shower water (which, by the way, i use a filter for and i highly recommend). i thought that wasn't fair, to be all lovey dovey with the water that i drink and not the water that i shower in. yea, i know, i'm a little different (laughs), but i don't ignore my shower water anymore, especially when i'm washing my hair (laughs), and i believe that all water should be acknowledged all the time. most importantly we should extend love and gratitude for its energy, for all that it does, for all that it is and for all that it's available for.

how dare you call it just hair?
when your hair is an extension of your nervous system
which consist of your brain, sensory organs and spinal cord
connecting to all that is within your being

when before you can even identify your environment
the strands of your hair have picked up the information
and communicated it to you
capable to inner-stand
capable of the reading

how dare you call it just hair?
when your hair is an antenna
transmitting and receiving signals from the atmosphere
gathering data that's connected to the cosmos

a magnetic organ
conduit to the etheric world
communicating with the ether
the sun and all of the universe
conducting energy into your body
increasing your vitality
absorbing and sending out your frequency
and attracting to you that very same vibe

how dare you call it just hair?
when it has many roles and is attached to living tissue
calling it dead protein--
combing it
pulling it
manipulating it
not being conscious of its true use

while all it wants to do is be of service to your body
instead of just appealing to the eye--
slathering it with dye

straightening it with lye
stop treating your hair as though it's dead
when, indeed, it's alive

how dare you call it just hair?
when it can send vitamins to your being
(*the longer and healthier it is*)
enhance your senses and intuition
send blood to sex organs
and provide you with what you didn't realize you needed

yet some of us allow it to become damaged
cutting it off
being abusive
not showing it love
as it displays signs of neglect

when all it wants to do is just be
be a part of your nervous system
that's powered by your own electricity
kink up
coil up
and be shown some respect

how dare you call it just hair?
when it's an organ that encases water
has consciousness and stores memory
while allowing anybody to touch it
as they transfer to you their energy

there is a network around your hair follicles
called the hair root plexus
that send and receive nerve impulses
to and from the brain when the hair moves
wanting you to be aware of it
as it is conscious of you

so you can benefit from its real use

how dare you call it just hair?
when it serves a purpose just like every other organ, gland
and system that makes you *you*
channeling solar and lunar energy
connecting with the life force around it
stimulating higher levels of consciousness
balancing your electromagnetic energy field
and keeping you in tune

all it wants to do is bring you nourishment
divine information
greater quantities of strength
insight
and assist you to tap into cosmic energy

so just let it be
and watch it be great for you

because it's more

than just hair

q. interesting poem, what made you write this one?

a. i was researching a lot about hair at the time, because something told me that it has to be there for more than just styling (laughs).

q. do you still feel the same way about hair?

a. for the most part, yes. i will say that it does serves a great purpose and has many benefits and uses when it's left alone. i mean yes, combing and washing the hair is cool (laughs), but try a wooden comb, try an all-natural shampoo with minimal ingredients. the hair is definitely an antenna and i'm sure it has even more functions than i am currently aware of.

be gentle with it, care for it naturally, let it breathe, and be mindful of who you let style your hair and their energy. and if you feel as though you need a fresh start and want to erase some memories, go on and chop it all off (laughs).

i got a brazilian wax today
not for nothing
but it hurt like hell
although not like the hurt previous sex partners left inside my womb

it may have only been 5 of them
4, 3, 2 or 1
but from all the mental cleansing
womb cleansing
and healing that was happening within my temple
something else still needed to be done

i thought to myself
if hair indeed stores memory
then i want to wax
strip
and remove the memories from my private parts
of those who shouldn't have ever got that close

i know sexual energy runs deeper than pubic hair
but i don't care
i felt liberated afterwards
it felt good to be bare

it felt good to be bare
knowing that my pubic hairs no longer have to be a container of energy from bad sex decisions i've made
i will allow them to grow back anew
to be born again
starting today

getting waxed was routine
but i would always leave a little in the middle
never hearing cries of *"please wax us too"*
so for the strip that felt left behind

when the other pubic hairs were being raptured
this too is for you

do i feel as though i have a clean slate?
maybe
and to whom it may concern
i don't really care if you find this crazy
all i know is that my vajayjay out here feeling like a new lady

i know hair grow out
and those energies may have already been trimmed off or shaved
but i needed those hairs ripped from their roots
i wanted nothing left behind
from past sex partners
all the way to the new

not sure if a brazilian wax truly helped
but it damn sure felt freeing
especially since a voice inside was what told me to do it

maybe it was my yoni
aware that i was starting a new journey
with a new look
and a new mindset
maybe she wanted to be included

i mean, girls cut their hair
and shave their heads after bad relationships all the time
and they feel liberated after as if all ties have been cut off

so why can't i do the same for my vagina?

2am
pain throbbing in my womb
i can't sleep
can barely move
i find the strength to get up

as i pace back and forth in the living room
with my hands touching the pain
i ask
what is it?
i am available
speak
tell me what is happening as i leak

i cry
but i don't reach for the tylenol
i cry
reaching for my pen
so my thoughts and how i feel i can write it all

i talk to my womb as the pain hits deep
was told that this pain i feel
is pain being released

fear
grief
trauma placed on the womb is leaving
the pain i feel is also ancestors celebrating all that i'm achieving
was once told that it's more than just blood that i'm bleeding
and my strength is necessary, *my strength is what's needed*

so i stay strong
as i cleanse the emotional debris that no longer serves me
or the generations before me and ahead
i stay strong
as my ancestors dance in my womb

stomping, twirling and clapping
as they push out the old and prepare me for what lies ahead

i stay strong
at 2am when the pain i can barely handle
but it's happening through me because the goddess
and my ancestors knew i would be able to handle
i stay strong

because at this point

that's all i'm able to do

what if the philosopher's stone is not a stone
but the blood that leaks from my womb
every time the moon is new?
an elixir of life
transforming mortality into immortality
full of genetic codes
regenerative stem cells of vitality

what if people used to worship the blood
that flowed from the womb
now some take pills in order to prevent it
or want their cycle to be over soon
that which flows from the divine sacred womb
is indeed the flower
the holy grail may indeed be the womb

when that time of the month comes
some complain of the aches and pain
and the cramps they gain
but what if they're just the cries from the divine feminine
desiring a deeper relationship
so that the goddess can further reign?

the blood which is full of memory
the blood that can intensify any intention that is honest
magical and healing
a living three-dimensional symbol
to remind all women of our connection to the mother goddess

rich with stories
rich in history
filled with wisdom
filled with mystery

dear moon blood
i intend to become more whole and aligned for you

i'll honor you and allow you to teach
the secretion is no longer a secret
the fruit of the tree of life flows through me

realizing and remembering that the blood from my womb
bonds me even further with the goddess
the goddess which represents the source
the goddess mother earth
the goddess i endorse

embracing the goddess
by embracing menstruation
the blood that is sacred
the blood that is powerful
the blood that should be celebrated
and utilized for its highest vibration

the blood that can be altered and enrich through intent
the blood i am grateful to experience
a sacred substance that i allow to flow every cycle
menstruation that i don't resent

the highest source of fertilization
filled with cosmic information
nurturing to earth
just like in the womb it was nurturing to us
by understanding and honoring the power of the blood
from the womb
the mother goddess will return
in full force
for us

the allower of all things
the glue
the heart
the generous

the source
the infinite that flows through this endless course

the blood that creates life
the feminine
the gift that can equip the masculine with sacred knowledge
and send him to other realms when intimate

the blood the gods once devoured
the flower
the blood that gives me strength
from day to day

it will never

ever

lose

its power

i put my hands on my womb
when she heals
i heal
we heal

Kia Marlene

when was the last time you talked to your womb?
told her how grateful you are for all that she does--
aligning your cycles according to the moon
allowing life to grow, be birthed and passed through you

permitting you to drip a substance every month
that was once considered an elixir of life desired by the gods
chances of you understanding your womb
and gaining a relationship with her
tell me the odds

do you care about your yoni at all?
or only when it's time for sex?
un-natural ingredients to her flesh
disrupting the ph balance, thinking its best

forget a summer's eve
give me the yoni steam
probiotics
unsweetened cranberry juice
coconut oil
and acv to stay fresh and heal myself if i ever need

do you care about your womb history?
her significance?
her health?
do you treasure her existence?

will you learn her physiology?
understand her energy centers?
take the time to heal emotional and sexual traumas?
will you be consistent?

i put my hands on my womb
and say i pledge to honor and cherish you
i pledge to send you my love

and my gratitude

i pledge to care for you naturally
talk to you
ask for forgiveness
and give you my attention

to overstand your power and our history
to bring you peace--
to keep you happy and balanced
is, indeed, my intention

vesica piscis
ankh
ram's head
holy grail
all of these are symbolic for you

home for the seeds to grow
gateway to this realm and others
you are all of these things too

she's conscious of you

so again

i ask

when was the last time you talked to your womb?

heal the womb
clear the womb
remove blockages
and open the womb
so that the frequency of love
can fill the womb

i rest

on the days i bleed from my womb
allowing the goddess to work overtime
distributing divine vibrations through my temple
respecting the flower that has bloomed

i rest

knowing that this natural biological cleansing
is accompanied by an emotional and psychological cleanse
which is accompanied by the opportunity
for me to let go of what no longer serves me
set intentions
and embrace the new

i rest

knowing that the hypothalamus
the pituitary gland
and my ovaries
have communicated and released hormones
which may have released information
which may have released visions
which may have released layers of the veil to be lifted
and created an opportunity for spiritual growth
for me to further overstand all that i embody
and for me to further get in tune

i rest

choosing not to block out any unconscious lunar information
which is reflective and intuitive
or any cosmic information that comes to me
resting so that i can listen and feel as my intuition is heightened

and as my dreams become more vivid and easier to decode
knowing that the right hemisphere of my brain
is more active during this time
and the solutions to any problems i have
i hold

i rest

knowing that i am dripping liquid wisdom
enlightenment
life-giving energy
ancient creative female power
immortality
healing
the fountain of life
i am dripping the souls of future and past generations

so i rest

and i ask my divine sacred womb
and the blood that it holds
then releases for me
to forgive me for the times
that i did not

from this day forward
when it's that time of the month

i

indeed

rest

i am a woman

i am the prize
heaven in between my thighs
galaxies in my eyes
able to give the toughest man butterflies
the strongest force there is
couldn't be torn down if other energies tried

i am a woman

whose womb is sacred just like the blood that flows from it
powerful
a living library
occupied by the souls of my ancestors and predecessors
seraphic frequency
a celestial being that operates out of love
without thinking anything of it

i am a woman

who can nurture the souls of broken men
who can heal her own temple
connect with the energy of the mother goddess
and access knowledge
just by going within

i am a woman

with the strength of a million males
the softest touch like chinchilla tails
i am the original
so my soul is filled with many tales

i am a woman

a protector and provider
can stand still or be a rider
be a lover or a fighter
transform darkness and make it lighter

i am a woman

who operates more from the right brain than the left
who can create joy when nothing is left
who was able to make myself whole again
when that man left

i am a woman

who overflows with emotions
yes i cry oceans
but i can alchemize my tears to give me vitality
and turn them into the most magical potion

i am a woman

whose heart is the sun
which radiates enough warmth
to heat up nations and keep things in tune
whose soul can fill rooms
whose energy causes things to bloom
whose womb is connected to the moon
and with every new cycle is a transformation
and the chance to become anew

i am a woman

the divine
the source
the feminine
magnetism

earth

the vessel that give birth to gods

i can create universes and destroy illusions
the universe dwells within me
as i dwell within it

i am a woman

and i am proud to be that

ode to my bedroom walls

i love these walls
they've heard my deepest thoughts
listened in on my secrets
witnessed my frustrations
had front row seats to my fears
they've heard my cries
felt my joy
they know all that i embody
are impressed with my love
touched by my sight
drenched in my energy
and not once have they judge
they've watched me grow
they've watched me transform
they watched me evolve
they've viewed my setbacks
and my comebacks
i love these walls
and i know they love me too

don’t tell me i’m trying to be something that i’m
not
when i have been all that there is

Kia Marlene

going through phases like the moon
i feel like i'm at the stage called new
everything seems dark
plus no answers coming through

setting intentions
trying to gain more wisdom
and more light
so i can be full like full moons

trying to gain more visions
and more sight
so i can see
even in dark rooms

went through the dark stages
fast forward now, light, i'm full of it
i'm glowing
illuminating the darkness
bringing people on this journey towards enlightenment
i hope they ready to embark this

all light
nothing dense
just a high frequency
grew in awareness
steady expanding
this time there will be no inconsistency

diving deep in the cosmic sea with no life jacket
waters talking to me saying "we got you"
information hitting me like a tidal wave
brain fully hydrated so the wisdom getting through

realized the gods left the keys for me to unlock many realities
so now i'm feeling like the locksmith of the multiverse

screaming i got the keys to other dimensions
had to unlock dormant parts of the brain
and activate dna strands to get them

regenerated and remembered who i was
no labels though because i'm infinite
my thoughts evolved
perception changed
so i don't discuss subjects that are limited
i stopped ingesting info that was designed to limit and control us
a long time ago
i'm out here trying to shift realities
a gifted soul
with gifted traits
i'm feeling real indigo

so what i'm saying is embrace the unknown
the unseen
in the midst of your dark period
your strength
your power
your light
will all increase

and the universe will guide you on how to carry it

and then it hit me

like a tidal wave
that i am the tidal and the wave
the strong winds that move swiftly
the volcano that erupts
and the earth that quakes

and then it hit me

i am not just a drop in the ocean
i am the drop and the ocean
i am the pebble that is thrown into the river
and the ripples that it creates
i am the river that the pebble is thrown into
and i am the sound of the splash that it makes

and then it hit me

as i felt the water splash
here i am
dripping in data
drenched in knowledge
absorbing wisdom
soaked in codes
saturated in intelligence

and then it hit me

we are not breathing in air
we are snorkeling through information
we are not standing
we are floating
and the birds don’t fly
they swim

and then it hit me

i am water
submerged in water
breathing underwater
communicating underwater
walking underwater
and talking underwater

and then it hit me

i am thought
i am light
i am water immersed in it all
swimming through days
that are not days
swimming through time and space
that's not time or space

and then it hit me

i was no longer drowning because i was aware
i was no longer struggling for air that was not there
i allowed my spine to flex in the deep end
i allowed my eyes to open
no veil
no goggles
so that my mind could get deep in

and then it hit me

to explore all parts of this cosmic sea
to explore all parts of eternity
to explore all parts that i am

to explore all parts that are me

sometimes i lay on my back
on my top porch
and stare at the sky
and ask the divine within me for a way out

how can i shoot through a sky that's not a sky
and pass by clouds that aren't real
and pass by the sun that they say is an illusion
and mesh with the one
mesh with the whole

how can i break free from this enclosure?
how can i break free from this dome?

jenny asked god to turn her into a bird so she can fly far away
well, i want to be turned into a dolphin so i can swim far away
so i can effortlessly swim through this cosmic ocean
and reach the shore

i want to be the 1st dolphin swimming the furthest
and when i reach the top where i can no longer be seen
i want to create the biggest splash as my head comes above water
i want to look around and say
"wow, another level
another plane"

sometimes i lay on my back
on my top porch
and stare at the sky
and ask the divine within me

for a way out

i'm from out of this world

i can feel it
i look at myself and notice that i don't fit in
my thoughts come from other dimensions
my body is a vehicle that wasn't supposed to be parked here

i can see the ether floating vertically around me
and when i ground myself to earth
my pituitary gland secretes extra hormones
which secretes extra messages
which reminds me

i'm from out of this world

my mind has become clear
all color has disappeared
i've been stretching my consciousness
to reach heights that aren't here
i see a connection between all things and i'm aware
i know this body is an electric battery so i charge it with care

my brain
has been overstimulated
since age 3
the power that resides in me
was active long before i plopped into this sea
my inward light has been over-illuminated
since i was in my mother's womb
before i was even able to see

i'm from out of this world

i am not human like i thought i was
this human suit is a disguise
i can alter my brainwaves with my eyes

my fire been erupted from the base of my spine
i remember falling into the wrong plane back in 89
i asked myself how can i rise out of this so many times

because

i'm from out of this world

applications
paper forms
surveys
and questionnaires
trying to keep us limited with labels like
what's your gender?
female or male?

or what's your ethnicity?
caucasian
african american
hispanic
asian
pacific islander
i'm like what the hell

where's the box i can check for being infinite?
where's the box i can check for being divine?
where's the box i can check for being hue-man?
or a multi-dimensional being able to transcend space and time?

don't you know labels were created to limit us
when we were created to be limitless?
don't you know that we are grand
and we shouldn't check boxes that downgrade our splendidness?

i am a spirit having a human experience
so if there isn't a box for that
then i choose not to specify

if there are only boxes to check for color
ethnicity
or gender
then i choose not to identify

i am never ending consciousness connected to all that there is
and grander than any label that they could create

so if i leave all boxes empty

it's probably because i'm unable to relate

am i apple?
is this body an apple device?
icloud the akashic records?
am i a phone?
iphone?

with icloud i can sign in, access and edit files
wondering how i can sign in
access the akashic records
and edit those files

access with intention maybe?
edit through perception maybe?

will the changes i make on this device
appear on all of my other devices?
other versions of me?
other realities that be?
is that why changing oneself
has changed everyone near and far to me?

being able to telepathically share information
with other forms that exist
making sure updated information is available
on all of my devices that exist

accessing it all
no matter if i choose to televise
accessing it all
no matter what device i choose to occupy

accessing all that's been stored
all thoughts that have been expressed
and all thoughts that have been hoard

synching from the brain all mental imagery

visual perceptions and illusions of this visual reality
and all i'm connected to
synching and having access
to all events, thoughts, information
and visions from the past, present
and the future of this earth plane
from high and low altitudes

i mean aren't i a vibration
converting acoustic vibrations
to electrical signals?
a telecommunication device
transmitting sound within and without over distance
sending and receiving information with a nervous system
carrying messages throughout the body
dispatching nerve impulses with no resistance

am i the computer?
is there an ipod
digital camera
and cellular phone all inside this human body?

am i apple?
is this body an apple device?
icloud the akashic records?
am i a phone?
iphone?

i am the gratitude that i feel
i am the love that i experience
i am the joy that overflows my being
i am the wealth that i accumulate
i am the abundance that i am in tune with
i am the bliss that's in my world
i am the peace that's in my mind
i am the balance that i once sought
i am the divinity that's within me

i am the oneness of the whole

i seem to be a verb
an action
a state of being
experiencing different states of being
an occurrence
an event
something that is happening
a phenomenon
motion
frequency
sound
i am not a person
place
nor thing
i am memory
light and water
floating within this cosmic sea
i am unknowable
i cannot be identified
i cannot be labeled
i cannot be categorized
i cannot be stable
i cannot be bound by time
i create worlds
i am the worlds that i create
i produce matter with my mind
i am the matter that i produce
i alter realities
i am the potter
the clay
and the creation
i can manifest with my thoughts focus and imagination
i cannot be named
i am nameless
colorless
genderless

and ageless
i am infinite
ongoing
endlessness
connected but unattached and cageless
i am energy within an environment that reflects itself
i am all that i see and all that i don't
i am thought
i am what precedes thought and what comes after it
i am everywhere
i am a spirit with a soul
connected to the whole
the macro and micro
i am not a person
place
nor thing
i am action
a state of being
experiencing different states of being
an occurrence
movement
i am an immortal
who can be morphed into other things
who can bring forth a different energy within different dreams
who will always reappear
who will always be here
and there
the source of creation is within me
and surrounds me
the me that is not me

i seem

to be

a verb

Evolution of Awareness

ancestors tell me
that the words i write
is for us and by us

they say
don’t worry
you’re included in the us

the bondage
from what we didn’t learn
or understand
you were born to free us

lifted the veil
expanded your awareness
did your temple work
then sought guidance
because you were born to reach us

reached out
connected and tapped in
because you were born to need us

transformed
nourished all of our existence
because you were born to feed us

told my ancestors that i realized i didn’t change for me

but i was born

to change

for us

she was a caterpillar
that didn't realize she could form wings
that didn't realize she could fly
she didn't realize she could change forms
so she never tried
she started realizing she was unlimited
and decided to just be
she evolved
formed wings
and began
to fly free

the caterpillar became the butterfly

just like a butterfly
we too can evolve

Kia Marlene

q. so the caterpillar became the butterfly?

a. indeed, indeed, the caterpillar most definitely transformed into a beautiful butterfly.

q. if you could change anything about this book, would you?

a. nope, not at all. although some of my views, opinions, theories and thoughts about certain topics has changed slightly, i still wouldn't go back and change a single poem. everything that i wrote and expressed in that very moment serves a purpose. it's a part of my evolution, it's a part of my growth, it's a part of my journey.

q. do you think your transformation will have an impact on others? do you think that your book will assist in anybody else's evolution of awareness?

a. i do know that my book changed me, and i do know that changing oneself is the beginning to changing everything else. so it is indeed my intention that my transformation and my book will have an impact on many, and assist in their own evolutions of awareness as well.

q. interesting. i can tell that you are very sincere about your intentions and wanting your transformation to help others along on their journeys. so i must, ask will there be another book after this one?

a. (sips water and smiles)

q. well, will there?

i am on a journey
a journey that will never end
a journey where i must consistently ask for guidance
a journey where i must ask for strength

it is crucial to be happy
it is crucial to stay focused
it is crucial to think for one's self
and to bloom like a lotus

many won't understand me
and i don't expect them to
many will criticize me
and i'll still respect those who do

all situations
and encounters
i've learned to embrace

all challenges
and fears
i've learned to face

i've discovered peace, joy
and love for all things
i've discovered my purpose, my power
and my divinity

all of these things that i discovered
were already within me and already here
i just had to become available
i had to become aware

on this journey
i am grateful to be on
and thankful for the direction from spirit that is sent

i am on a journey

a journey that will last for eons

a journey that will never end

this story never ends

and neither do yours

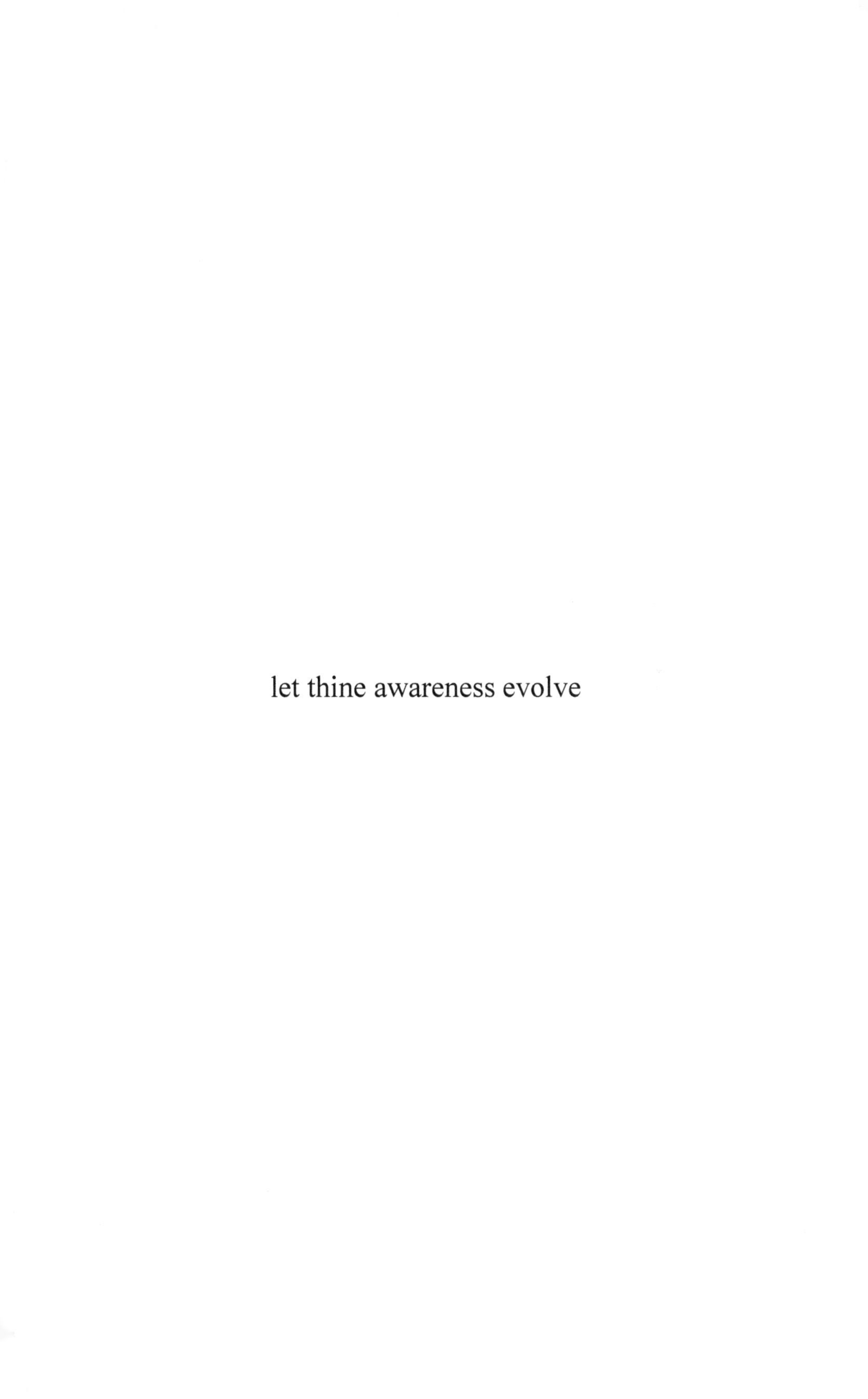

let thine awareness evolve

Bonus
(knock knock)

q. knock knock?

a. yes, these next few poems are all knock knock poems, inspired by a young boy named zyiere parker whose energy can easily light up any room. last summer, when i started writing this book, every time i ran into him he would come up to me and say “knock knock” and i would respond with the usual “who’s there”, and then he would respond with a sentence about how his day was or what happened in school. he did this for about a week straight, every time i saw him (laughs). i guess the knock knock stayed with me, because it inspired me to write a few poems.

knock knock
“who’s there?”
“forgiveness”
“forgiveness who?”
“forgiveness,
middle name joy
last name inner peace
yes it’s been awhile
so may we come in and talk, please?”

when was the last time you forgave?
when was the last time you freed your heart from resentment
and allowed joy to come your way?

did you know that if you allow for forgiveness
you allow for healing?
did you know that if you forgive
you will be filled with inner peace
and your joy will be appealing?

so let’s change it up

resentment
bitterness
pain
anger

let’s hang it up

we will get you a new wardrobe
because joy will look good on you
your smile will compliment your style
and inner peace will glow on you

forgiveness will also glow on you
because forgiveness equal strength

forgiveness will open doors
and create opportunities
that will reach many heights
and lengths

so open your door
and allow us
forgiveness
inner peace
and joy
to come in
we want to introduce you to true happiness and healing

a journey that begins within

knock knock
“who’s there?”
“gratitude”
“gratitude?
oh yea, i think i’ve heard of you”

well i was hoping you had--
when was the last time you gave thanks
for all of the things that you have?

are you even grateful for your experience here on earth?
do you not acknowledge the good
and only complain about the bad?
do you understand the power of gratitude?
do you even know the half?

did you know gratitude can open doors?
and when you’re grateful for all the good in your life
you will receive more

gratitude can eliminate the negative
and increase the positive
gratitude can bring forth happiness
and happiness is indeed the prerogative

so be grateful for the now
be grateful for the past
be grateful for the things you want
but don’t yet have

believing is seeing
so be grateful for all you desire
believe it is already here
give thanks

and watch manifestations transpire

knock knock
"who's there?"
"love"
"love who?"
"love who?
i'm all that there is
so if you don't know me then that's a problem
have any troubles or issues?
then i'm the main ingredient to solve them

but first let me ask you this
do you have love for yourself?
did you know that loving who you are
is loving everything else

i am one of the greatest
most powerful forces in this universe
so what do you mean you don't put me first?

you may not be able to see me
but i'm something you can feel
i am a divine power
a positive force
i am needed and, indeed, real

did you know that if you give and let love in
you can fill yourself with it?
you are love
so it's time you start revealing it

it's time you start releasing it
it's time you start being it
still not a fan of love?
then i guess you won't be seeing it

and i'm not just talking about loving your family and friends

you must love yourself
and all that there is
love is the cure
and that which isn't pleasant in your life
is the sickness

so express love and give love
towards every situation
and all things around you will improve

soon you will witness

fall in love with the journey
fall in love with life
fall in love with you

Kia Marlene

acknowledgements
to lau'ren mcghee, my book would not be complete without the beautiful cover you provided me with, i am beyond grateful. to caitlin conlon, your eyes are a gift, you are extremely special and i am very appreciative. to my supporters, i am truly grateful for you all, from the bottom of my heart, i say, thank you.

CPSIA information can be obtained
at www.ICGtesting.com
Printed in the USA
BVHW081540251022
650236BV00007B/273